EMPOWER YOUR LIFE

EMPOWER YOUR LIFE

A GUIDE TO YOUR HIGHEST PURPOSE

BY PREM SADASIVANANDA

ISBN: 978-1-54392-079-6

TABLE OF CONTENTS

Dedication

I dedicate this token of gratitude to the great master, Swami Sivananda, and to my guru, Swami Vishnu-devananda, whose teachings, love and unceasing presence continue to inspire and fill my life with hope, love and wisdom. It is only through their grace that this book could have taken birth.

I also make this offering to the International Sivananda Yoga Vedanta Centers, the organization in which I lovingly served for over twenty-four years and which trains and inspires thousands of those in search of Light.

Acknowledgments

Books are born in mysterious ways. An inspiration arises in our heart, our heart receives the resonance, we make an effort to tune to the particular message we have received, and there we are—the book is in your hands!

This book is the outcome of the numerous courses I taught over many years on the subjects of Positive Thinking, Meditation and Vedanta Philosophy during my service as a swami in the Sivananda Yoga Vedanta Organization.

I would like to thank all the students of the Sivananda Organization who were the instruments in my growth as a teacher, and especially to the students who attended the experimental six-month course on Positive Thinking, which took place at the Sivananda Yoga Center, New York.

My very special gratitude goes to:

Dawn Bossman (Bharati) and Penny Collie (Padmavati) for their untiring work on giving this book a form that is fully alive and inspirational!

And to Ania Sluchak (Purna Devi) for her lovely design and elegant artistic touch!

Prem Sadasivananda

Asato Mā Sat Gamaya
Tamaso Mā Jyotir Gamaya
Mṛtyor Mā'mrtāt Gamaya

Lead me from the unreal to the Real
Lead me from darkness to Light
Lead me from mortality to Immortality

(Bhrihadaranyaka Upanishad 1.3.28)

A glorious brilliant future is awaiting you.
Let the past be buried.
You can work miracles; you can do wonders.

Swami Sivananda

CHAPTER I

LIVE TO FEEL INSPIRED

Your life is the expression of the limit of your thoughts. There is no greater joy than that of contemplating and seeing life as the most precious gift and living life with inspiration and the right purpose. But what does it mean to be inspired? It means to fly on the wings of hope and gratitude, to have a dream, to cherish an ideal and live with a purpose that inspires and enriches every single moment of our life and which will lift us to the not-yet-imagined heights of our potential and spirit.

The first step on this beautiful journey of life is to awaken our inspiration. To have inspiration means to kindle deep faith within oneself—faith in the order of the universe, in the laws that are behind all Creation which sustain all beings, in our own strength and potential, and faith above all in the power of love. To be inspired is to rouse oneself from the sleep of mediocrity. Let your heart feel the stirring of life within and be impelled by the power of your ideals. Let your dreams translate your deepest convictions, your inner force, your greatest love into the most palpable reality—your own life, the life that also becomes the inspiration for the lives of others.

Inspiration is the quality of the heart; it is the fire of spirit that burns itself into the subtle psychic matter, creates forms and molds the seemingly formless energy into visible creations. Envision the quality of inspiration as an ever-running stream of energy that gives direction, meaning and the necessary impetus for your life. It is this inspiration accompanied with deep faith that animates our thoughts, words and actions. There will be magic in your look that will help others find their own inspiration. Inspiration is but another name for love. We feel inspired by what we love. To kindle such inspiration we need to tune into and align ourselves with the source of all inspiration. The Divine within us will give a greater vision and will lead us to great accomplishment in life. Those who are inspired are able to actualize their vast potential now, at this very moment.

Once awakened keep the fire of inspiration burning ever brightly in your heart! One whose inspiration is alive is young even though old in age. And one whose inspiration has dried up and gone from the heart is as if no longer living. Become the author of your own destiny. Awaken the inspiration and put to use your willpower. You will soon discover the source of all light, all joy and all life. That source is none other than your own heart. The medium through which you arrive at the source is the application of the best and the finest of your thoughts, actions and words. Such a way of life is no less than what we may call a Divine life on this planet earth; it is the most sublime life indeed.

Have you ever thought that you could be living a much richer life, a life that thrives beyond the ordinary, mediocre and prosaic? Is it possible to see in life the light, joy and love even in darkness and difficult moments? It is possible! Have you contemplated deeply on what is beyond this apparent reality called ordinary life? Doesn't the word 'ordinary' imply that there is also something extraordinary? Yes! Your life is meant to be extraordinary. We attain what we aspire to, what our vision extends to. Our life is the direct result of our vision. What power or force do we need to tap into in order to achieve the greatest and the fullest of our life? The power of our thoughts.

Where and how we do we begin planting the seeds of who we would like to become and the life we would like to live? We begin by learning to harness the power of our thoughts. On deeper analysis we come to realize that our life is nothing but the manifestation of our thoughts. Not more, not less. Just as a building is made of bricks and mortar, so is our life made up of the material of our thoughts. But there is something beyond the thoughts—it is the essence of life as pure existence, pure consciousness and bliss. Every created thing has a thought behind it and this is true even for our body. The power behind all that is created is the creative power of thought. The knowledge of the power of thought is the greatest knowledge indeed. We are about to discover and explore the incredible world of the mind.

Our greatest power, our ability to create by means of thought, is neglected and underestimated. We think lightly of the power of thought until we experience its full force. When we experience acute mental anguish or we are intensely focused and the power of thought surges within us, we begin to see that the power of thought and the ability to concentrate are interlinked and interdependent.

Thoughts are the essential building blocks of who we are and what we experience. We have countless possibilities and ways of making and remaking ourselves into anything we want. The power is available to us to mold our habits and our character, to attract the right conditions for our evolution. We can develop the unseen potential of the mind, utilize this power for the service of humanity and so influence the world we live in for the better. There is a bright future for all those who are willing to train their minds and learn to consciously exercise and direct their thought power.

We are the witnesses of what thought can create in the material world, but we have not yet experienced the dawning of humanity's bright future, which will occur once we have understood the importance of right thought. Our experiences in life are meant to help us discover our strength. It is only our negative thoughts and erroneous concepts that hold us back from realizing our goals and dreams.

Life is an endless stream of beginnings that may be right or wrong depending on our power of discrimination and belief. All right beginnings have their origin in positive and constructive thinking. Let your dreams come true! By harnessing the mind's power you can create your destiny. You can arm yourself against challenges and difficulties. You can make your difficulties into stepping-stones to success.

Once upon a time, after hearing an inspiring talk by a wise man, a woman approached him and said, "I feel very inspired by what you have just said. I would love to go deeper into my practice and follow my spiritual path, but my life is full of obstacles." The wise man asked, "What obstacles do you have?" The woman replied, "Well, I am married, I have two children and work hard all day long, and on top of it, I take care of my sick mother. I have no time to do my spiritual practice, to meditate or even think positively. These obstacles seem insurmountable." The wise man was indeed wise! He said, "There is one thing, madam, that you don't see . . . the obstacles are the path!"

Whatever your 'obstacle' may be—your health, relationship, job or even all these, you can look at them as opportunities for your own quantum leap of positive change and ultimately for your spiritual awakening. Different people are given different obstacles as their path. There may be someone in your family who is an alcoholic, or you may recently have been through a bad relationship, or you might be suffering from a challenging disease or a difficult financial situation. Know for sure that there is a positive purpose behind the challenge and that you can turn any or all of those experiences into the tools for your self-mastery and freedom. Don't wait for the waves in the ocean to subside before you swim. Jump into the ocean of life and become victorious now!

The choice is yours! The choice has to be made now, this very day! Our choices have much less to do with our circumstances and much more with the power of our own will and the clarity of purpose. Frequently we see how those who are strong, when they experience difficult situations, are in fact invigorated by them and are motivated to excel and rise above their temporary limitations by the challenge itself. Our attitude has a bearing on every situation in our life. Or put simply: attitude is everything. Take this to be the absolute truth. Attitude is the representation of our deepest strength and is the source of numerous possibilities that lie dormant within our spirit. Cultivate the attitude that life works always in your favor, that it labors for you whether you know it or not, and with this right attitude transform every challenge into an opportunity for growth and awakening. Miracles happen daily, and if we are alert enough we will see that countless opportunities and the greatest magic lie in the tiniest of moments. The most beautiful flowers grow in the compost along a dusty road. We can be compared to wild flowers that emanate the most beautiful fragrance in all conditions. Your mind is your garden. It is up to you what seeds you want to see blossom there.

All things are possible to those who believe in the possibility. Become a staunch believer in self-reliance and self-effort. You can determine your fate by force of thoughts. As clouds are the main source of rain, so the control of one's own thoughts is the source of durable prosperity. You are yourself your own friend or enemy. If you will not save yourself by cherishing good thoughts, there is no other remedy.

Swami Sivananda

True spiritual teaching is practical; it is about self-empow-erment. None but our own purest, most loving thoughts and intentions can help us. Take rest in the garden of your most beautiful thoughts. Find strength in your inner light and joy. Live all the possibilities of your transformation in this very moment. To change one's thoughts requires a commitment like no other. Positive and creative thinking is an art as well as science. It is the art of all arts and, more importantly, the art of living in wisdom, peace and love.

EXERCISE
A CONTEMPLATION FOR AWAKENING INSPIRATION

Contemplate daily for a few minutes:

- Can you evoke any memories of times when you felt very inspired? Bring them on! Let yourself feel the same inspiration now!

- What does inspiration feel like? What is its quality or energy? Where does it well up from?

- What would be necessary to sustain the inspiration throughout the day, or even for life? What would be its source?

- Where does your heart go to most often? Is there a place within your mind where you like to go daily in search of inspiration and rejuvenation?

- If you had the resources, the time, the energy, the extra support, what is it that you would love to do the most? Link that idea to what you think your greater purpose in life is, general or ultimate.

- Every creation has a seed. What is the seed of human life? What are the best seeds of who you are?

CHAPTER 2

THE NATURE OF THOUGHT—
AS YOU THINK SO YOU BECOME

Thought is ancestor of action. If you want to improve your actions purify your thoughts.

Swami Sivananda

We live on the wings of possibility. Every being is in its deepest essence pure and perfect. All beings are made in the image of the great Creator and therefore are essentially divine. But in order for that divinity to unfold we must know, understand and master ourselves. And until we gain mastery over ourselves—the mind, to put it more precisely—we can neither know our true Self as the one Pure Awareness, nor the powers of our mind in all their glory. The mind is power, energy in itself, and it needs to be harnessed properly for it to become a perfect tool of liberation and freedom.

Lord Krishna in the Bhagavad Gita says:

Let one raise oneself by oneself alone; may one not let oneself down; for verily one's own self alone is the friend of oneself, and oneself alone is one's own enemy.

Bhagavad Gita, Ch VI v. 5

Our mind carries the capacity for being the cause of liberation as well as of bondage and delusion. In reality we have neither enemies nor friends outside of ourselves. Our enemies exist in the form of unconquered and unrestrained negative thoughts and emotions that appear to take the form of the external conditions, situations and people that we encounter. Our true enemies are fear, anger, hatred, greed, lust, jealousy and unnecessary and selfish desires that have been allowed to grow like weeds. Thankfully, we have friends—in the form of positive intentions and thoughts, our compassion and our selfless heart filled with abundant love—who are able to accomplish wonderful things for us and others in this world and beyond.

Have we not witnessed the power of our mind, positive or negative, in our lives? Yes, we have! And we have most likely discovered that when our mind is in a negative state, it surrenders its powers and becomes the victim of circumstance. And when we are at the height of our inspiration and strength we demonstrate the tremendous power of spirit within us and become the active creators of our own lives.

Spiritual life in its essence is nothing but working with our thoughts. Spirituality means being awakened to the power of our mind, to the fact that our thoughts are the most creative force in the universe. And it is the immensity of the power of this creative force that astonishes us. We see how our thought world unfolds to us as different types of reality, each one more confounding than the next.

Once we realize that spiritual life consists primarily in gaining control over our moods, emotions, thoughts and imagination, our focus in life shifts from looking for the best environment and conditions to finding the right method of working with the mind. Then we acquire the power of will and strength to guide our mind in the direction of truth and peace. Our life is built from within and a new life can be created by cultivating new thoughts and ideas. Our heart, the repository of the deepest thoughts and beliefs, keeps fashioning our external life according to the quality of these thoughts. Moment by moment let your most powerful, purest, choicest thoughts be strung on the rosary of your life.

We are all living, so to speak, in a vast ocean of thought; and the very atmosphere around us is continually filled with the thought-forces that are being continually sent or that are continually going out in the form of thought-waves. We are all affected more or less by these thought-forces either consciously or unconsciously and in the degree that we are more or less sensitively organized or in the degree we are negative and so are open to outside influences, rather than positive, which thus determine what influences shall enter into the domain of our thoughts and hence into our lives.

Swami Sivananda

Thoughts are the building material of the physical universe in which we live. Life is a visible manifestation of the power of thought. In this divine theater, behind the screen of life, thoughts are the real actors and the managing director of the play is the Divine Self or Consciousness.

The events in our lives are nothing but solidified forms of our thoughts—they are only the outer shell of our thinking. All materialization is preceded by thought. Most of us have very little understanding of what causes life to happen in the way it does. And when we don't understand the whys and hows we tend to ascribe them to capriciousness. In reality nothing is accidental, nothing happens by chance. Whether we win the lottery, enjoy unalloyed success, meet our life partner, stumble onto the spiritual path, or whether there is an earthquake or hurricane, everything happens according to the precise law of thought. Events are the result of the fine operations of the subtlest forces in the universe—thoughts. And our life, in fact the whole universe, is simply a mathematical presentation of them.

Thoughts are often regarded as fleeting and intangible ideas, abstract entities, the result of brain activity or intellectual activity, with no substance, and with a nature that cannot be objectified in any way. And even though their effect is measurable in life, it is hard for many of us to say what thoughts are exactly. Thoughts seem ethereal, insubstantial and transient. This approach to the nature of thought has developed alongside the materialistic attitude toward life that now dominates most of the Western world. A similar position is upheld today with regard to the nature of the mind. Many are of the opinion that the brain and mind are one and the same. The masters of spiritual traditions say categorically that they are not the same.

The basic nature of thought is that of vibration and it is made up of an extremely fine substance. As vibration, it behaves like a wave. Thoughts are subtle and imperceptible to the ordinary human mind. We can think of them as forces, vibrations, energies, living entities with a particular substantiality in them. Because of their wave-like nature they are called vrittis, known as thought waves in yoga. To understand how they operate we can visualize thoughts using the image of a pebble thrown into a calm lake, producing ripples or concentric circles that arise from the point of disturbance. Similar types of ripples emanate from the mind. Physical reality is permeated by a more refined reality or substance called manas, the mental atmosphere, in which thoughts exist and travel far and wide in all directions. When a thought arises in the mind, it gives rise to the vibrations in the mental atmosphere as a ripple effect and sends similar vibrations to the minds of others.

Thoughts are a form of matter; the qualities that we see in objects are also present in thoughts although in a much more subtle form. Just as a physical object has size, color, texture and weight amongst others, thoughts also possess such qualities. They also have a particular power. Thoughts create a form of matter similar to a thin vapor which is just as real as the air around us. Great spiritual masters and those who are psychically sensitive are able to perceive some or all of these qualities. Even animals and plants feel the thoughts around them. On a lower level of vibration even than thought, a pet will respond to the subtle vibration of an object, food or person, rather than to what we understand to be smell or sight. In fact tastes, smells and colors are nothing but the manifestation of the subtle essence of what is called prana in yoga, which can be loosely translated as vital energy. When we eat our favorite fruit we are assimilating its prana. Its qualities are simply a manifestation of the energy contained in the fruit. Thoughts are the most subtle form of prana, or energy.

When the mind is completely calm and free from thought there is an absence of name, form or object. As soon as thought begins to manifest it immediately takes a name (sounded in our mind as words) and a form. Thus every thought has a certain name, a word related to it, and a form. Form is the more refined state and the word or name is the grosser state of the same manifesting power. In fact the three are one. If we think of a thought as a form of energy, then the thought, form and word are nothing but the different vibratory levels of a single energy wave.

Thought lies in the astral body, one of three bodies we have, along with the physical and the causal (the cause of the other two). Our mind has a psychic manifestation in the form of an aura. The aura shows the structure of our astral body, particularly the mental and emotional components. The purpose of the aura is manifold. It is our means of communication with various cosmic forces and—just like the skin on our body— acts as a deterrent to negative forces, preventing them from entering and influencing our mind and body. It also serves as an antenna for beneficial influences to enter and nourish our being. Negative thoughts such as worry, depression, lust, greed and hatred are known to produce a 'crust' or dark layer on the surface of the mind or astral body. This crust, which looks like dirt, prevents the entry of beneficial influences and allows the negative forces or lower influences to operate upon the mind and the body. Psychological states are generally created or influenced by the presence or entry of certain forces.

In order to better understand the nature of thought, let us explore some of its qualities.

Velocity

The greater the level of subtlety of an object or energy, the greater and more powerful its nature and the faster its speed. Being the subtlest of forces, thoughts move with tremendous speed. We cannot imagine the speed of thought, next to which even the speed of light is slow. It takes eight minutes for light to reach from the sun to Earth, but it takes less than a second for our mind (as thought) to 'touch' the sun. We know from experience that thoughts form in a fraction of a moment.

We see objects but we do not understand how we see them. Our perception is serial, not instant, even though it appears to be so. Our mind conjures up images and sense impressions bit by bit, percept by percept into what we may call a perception. The mind does not perceive or take images in the way that a camera does. The camera takes the whole picture in a moment. But the mind forms single perceptions and we generate images through a process that is similar to, and that moves like, the frame-by-frame movement of a film in predigital movie-making. The tremendous speed at which the mind moves forms the solid image of the object perceived. Without this speed of thought there would be no such thing as perception of solidity. In addition, yoga teaches that we can only have one thought at a time in the mind. How multitasking works will be explained later in the book.

Study the mind and you will be amazed to see how it creates and perceives. It is only through the play of the mind upon objects that time appears to be either short or long, and space appears to be far or near. The objects in this world are in fact unconnected; they are connected and associated together only by thought, by the imagination of the mind. It is the mind that clothes objects with their apparent colors, shapes and qualities. In the Yoga Sutras of Patanjali we are reminded that the mind assumes the shape of any object upon which it thinks intensely. Every form of experience from the gross to the most subtle, every object, and every person is formed by the power of our thought. Each one of us creates a world of good and evil, pleasure and pain, only from our own imagination. These qualities are not inherent in objects or people; they belong to the attitude and imagination of our mind. The power of the mind is indeed awesome!

Color

Color represents a thought force. The colors of thought belong to a different dimension of perception and can be perceived in the aura by those who have psychic vision. They have many different hues and shades. For example, when we are happy and feeling content, when our intentions are positive and selfless, thoughts will have bright, clean colors and are well-defined. Spiritual thoughts are golden. Thoughts of depression are dark, heavy, black and murky. Thoughts of selfishness are brownish in color. The color of anger is red. Note that wearing certain colors stimulates thoughts related to the qualities associated with them. The human aura has permanent features in it as well as fast-changing colors corresponding to the thoughts of its owner. The colors in our aura vary according to our physical, mental, ethical and spiritual development.

Yellow resembles the color of the sun and denotes intellect. It is a color of inspiration, optimism and enthusiasm. It signifies the level and quality of intellectual development. It indicates the level of truthfulness, self-development, the power of discrimination and grasping (understanding), the power and quality of concentration and of willpower. In short, it represents the level of general intelligence. Capable and deep thinkers such as scholars, researchers, philosophers, scientists, wise people and those whose level of spiritual understanding and scholarship is high have a column-like shape of yellow in their aura. However, if there is an influence or mix of other colors, this generally indicates that their knowledge has been compromised by jealousy, pride, falseness or ambition, or their knowledge is incomplete or purely theoretical. If the intellectual development is directed toward a lower type of activity or study the yellow is dull; when directed towards spiritual realization, or the study of spiritual scriptures, it has a clear, golden color.

Wearing yellow stimulates the development of spirituality and discrimination. It fosters the awakening of spiritual impressions in the mind and improves the functions of understanding and teaching. The ancients in India knew about the power and influence of wearing particular colors. Children at a certain age were initiated into the Gayatri mantra and wore yellow clothing. Gayatri represents the sun, Divine Knowledge. The sun represents the intellect. The astral color of the intellect is yellow. To wear yellow was to influence this unfoldment. Yellow stimulates what is known as tejas, or brilliance of aura. Yellow is beneficial for both teachers and students.

Orange, a combination of yellow and red, has a variety of meanings depending on the exact tone and shade. It is a dynamic color and more complex to analyze since it can represent good health, the basic drives, sensuality, warmth, pride and/or ambition. It can also signify joy and happiness, or fire. Hindu swamis (monks) wear orange to represent the fire of purification.

Red is powerful, warming, stimulating and energizing and in its many variations indicates different qualities. If clear it represents vigor, vitality, virility, friendship, love of companion-ship, love of physical exercise or passion. Crimson or rose-like colors represent affection and non-sensual love. Scarlet, in the shape of arrows or flames indicates anger. Black with red sug-gests base sensuality accompanied with darkness and brutal-ity. Thoughts in the shape of red arrows set in green signify anger mixed with jealousy. When red leans toward pink it is a sign of greater sensitivity and of artistic tendencies.

Green represents life, balance, tact, politeness, love of nature, sense of sacredness, healing, calmness, adaptability, sympathy, ability to communicate well, charity, travel and intelligence. Spending time in nature helps nurture these qualities. Green with tones of brown represents jealousy. Dark green suggests diplomacy or cunningness and greenish tones may indicate thoughts of envy. Muddy green can be a sign of blame and struggles with taking responsibility. Dark green with gray de-notes deceit.

Blue is of a higher frequency and indicates thoughts and sen-timents of devotion, faith, peacefulness, morality, and psychic qualities such as clairvoyance and spirituality.

Brown when clear denotes avarice, miserliness and greed. When earthy tones are present it may represent one who has a grounding quality, or one who works with the earth.

Gray has a very low frequency. When clear it suggests low self-esteem and a closed spirit. If it is tinged with brown and appears dull it represents stagnation of energy and selfishness. A deep and heavy gray indicates depression and negativity. Gray is also associated with fear. Interestingly, the face turns pale in intense fear.

Black, also of very low frequency, signifies emotions such as hatred and malice. Combined with dark red it denotes base sexuality, passion and gloom, and is often used in places to stimulate such thoughts.

Violet represents the presence of the highest ideals in the soul: intuition, healing powers, prayerful and meditative qualities indicating the highest religious sentiments.

White, when clear, strong and radiant represents purity, and at times the highest spiritual realization, the supreme development of Consciousness.

Silver is a manifestation of spiritual qualities and at times, contact with angels.

Gold reveals wisdom and great spiritual realization.

Weight
When we are happy we feel light and elated and when depressed and worried, heavy. We use expressions such as, "I feel weighed down," or "I feel I have a great weight on my shoulders." Joy has lightness and so do thoughts related to actions with pure and selfless motives, thoughts of love and prayerful thoughts.

Shape or Form
Japanese scientist Dr. Masaru Emoto has shown in his experiments that thought has the power to alter the molecular structure of matter. The more spiritual, kind and selfless a thought, the more beautiful is the geometric shape. The more negative the thought, the more inharmonious the shape. This also holds true in different forms of the arts where artists project the quality of their thoughts onto the canvas, paper or screen. Prayerful thoughts have soft, rain-like forms and can take on beautiful halo shapes. Anger manifests as red arrows travelling towards a target. Crooked, deceptive or greedy intentions evince as little hooks or arms, crooked in shape, emanating outwards. Thoughts of healing, joy and inspiration have an-

gel-like shapes which flutter around us; thoughts of depression, worry and negativity have heavy cloud-like forms.

Size

Thought forms can be small or large. Thought can be limited and narrow or expansive and grand. Compassion, empathy, large-heartedness, big-thinking all indicate expanded thoughts. Small-mindedness, shallow thinking, short sightedness suggest a closed and diminished mind.

When prayers are offered in a gathering, with devotional charge and with deep concentration, large thought forms are generated. During spiritual gatherings the minds of those meditating and praying together attract magnitudes of luminous entities and light.

Negative thoughts emanating from a large number of people create negative cloud-like thought forms of enormous size.

Direction

As with all force in the material world thoughts travel and can be directed to a specific person or country. Those who have a strong will or desire can easily project their thoughts through space, often to a great distance. All forces in nature need a medium or a vehicle through which they can move; for example sound needs air. How can we explain the movement of thought through space, or from one mind to another? The answer is that the subtle manas or mind-substance or mental atmosphere fills all space and serves as the vehicle or medium for thought. We say, "I am sending you beautiful thoughts." We see from the rituals of different spiritual traditions that mediums such as water or fire can be charged by thoughts and are used for transmission of powerful intentions.

Life Span

Thoughts are living entities and are endowed with a life force with its own life span. Thoughts which lack depth, intensity, concentration or willpower have a short life span, while others, nurtured over time by individuals or societies, can survive for hundreds or even thousands of years. The effects of thoughts of those who have lived before us can still be felt. They may be a source of great blessings, or have a negative effect on the world. Even though yesterday's thought influences us to a greater or lesser extent, through will power today's thoughts can gradually supplant the thoughts from the past.

Sensing Thought

Even though thoughts generally cannot be seen, they can still be felt, sometimes consciously. We feel others' thoughts, even viscerally, as if the current of their thought was passing through us. It is easier to feel the thoughts of those in close proximity. When someone happy sits next to us we can sense their lightness and joy. Their joyful aura is touching our aura. At other times we can feel quite uncomfortable, manifesting as little prickles or as a 'creepy feeling', if another has angry, deceitful or unwanted lustful thoughts towards us.

Our doors to life are wide open. Our life shines with manifold possibilities. Knowing that our thoughts are more real than we ever imagined and that they are infused with such great potential we can now employ their power to bring about positive changes in our own and other peoples' lives. Clearly we are the creators of our own destiny.

CHAPTER 3

THE INFLUENCE OF THOUGHT

The power of thought depends upon the strength with which it has been projected. Our ability to send a powerful beam of thought depends on our level of concentration and the degree of our psychic and spiritual development. Few of us are able to put much force behind our thoughts because our thinking has become mechanical. For thoughts to be powerful they require the living force of awareness and intention behind them. Think and send only good thoughts. The grand Law of Affinity or 'Like attracts like', is one of the main principles in the operation of thought.

If you entertain a negative thought, that thought attracts all sorts of negative thoughts from other people. You pass on those thoughts to others also. Thought moves. Thought is a living dynamic force. Thought is a thing. If you allow your mind to dwell on a sublime thought this thought will attract good thoughts from others.

Swami Sivananda

When we think a thought we create a living entity that takes on a life of its own. An ocean of thought surrounds us and we are adding to this ocean by the quality of our thoughts. We are continuously attracting certain thoughts and repelling others. The law that operates within the thought world is the Law of Affinity—"Like attracts like". Thoughts attract other thoughts that are similar in nature and character. Thoughts get together, coalesce, reinforce and amplify each other—birds of a feather flock together. Thoughts are psychic magnets. Every thought attracts to itself a thought of similar character. The greater the effort we put into cultivating positive thoughts the greater the support we will receive from those who also have positive thoughts as well as from those who are more evolved beings.

Whatever thought or desire we hold in our mind will attract—consciously or unconsciously—that particular thought to ourselves, whether a person or a condition of life. Thoughts draw to themselves particles of astral matter from different strata of thought worlds and become as if wrapped in a mantle, growing heavier and more defined as they do so. They gradually descend into matter and materialize in the form of experiences, circumstances and beings which enable us to experience the effects of the thoughts. Our mind has acted as a magnet for certain vibrations that have now taken the form of a tangible reality that acts upon us like a boomerang. Every so-called blessing or curse is the result of our thought vibration. Circumstances simply reveal themselves to us through the medium of our thoughts.

The more intensely we think of something the more real it becomes. In this manner with the many thoughts not only in this lifetime, but also from previous lifetimes, we attract to ourselves situations and people according to our dominant thoughts. This forms our relationship with the world in which we live. By virtue of the power of thought we have a great responsibility as human beings. Every thought we have contributes either to the happiness and well-being or to the pain and suffering, for both ourselves and for the world. Imagine the mind as a satellite, and the minds of others as satellites also. When we project thought it instantly makes contact with other 'satellites' before it returns to us.

If we develop an interest, for example in playing music, we will set in motion thoughts that attract similar thoughts. Soon we will hear about music teachers, books, websites, and places where we will be able to materialize our desire to play music.

If we entertain low, selfish thoughts we open ourselves to thought forms of similar character which already exist and 'lurk' in the psychic atmosphere. Such mental influences can take hold of our minds, alter our usual positive thinking and urge us on to act in ways that we would have shrunk from doing previously. Any unusual behavior that is out of character for one who is habitually positive and selfless indicates the presence of such entities and thoughts. We have the right to invite whatever influences we want into our mind and there are all kinds of mental 'guests' out there in the vast ocean of thought. But let us always invite in inspirational guests that will help us in our evolution!

Thoughts form levels or strata in astral space, just as clouds form groups of clouds in the atmosphere. However this does not mean that each stratum of thought occupies a certain portion of space to the exclusion of others. For example, space remains intact even though many kinds of waves travel through it at any given moment. Thought vibrations are of different degrees, and the same thought-space may be filled with thought matter of thousands of varieties with no interference or communication between them. Just as several people can dream in the same room and there will be no connection between their dream worlds, so also we can experience an individual reality of our own with no reference to the reality of others. Each one of us continually creates our own individual world.

If we nurture positive thoughts they will influence the minds of other beings with similar thoughts, adding to the realization of their intentions. Similarly, a negative thought will affect others with a similar thought structure causing them to act negatively. A mere thought could become just what another needs in order to accomplish either a positive or negative deed.

The law of affinity operates also internally within our own mind. We find that virtues tend to attract one another. If we practice kindness on a regular basis, we will also start to practice patience, truthfulness and other virtues. Vices flock together too. One who succumbs to the habit of lying may start to steal or cheat, leading to a downward spiral. Cultivate positive thoughts such as kindness, courage, love and purity and the negative thoughts will perish by themselves. Those with similar types of thoughts unconsciously gravitate towards one another. Our friendships are based on this law.

Thoughts charge objects, places, substances, and living beings. For this reason too we keep objects given to us by our loved ones. The influence of thought does not necessarily diminish when a person leaves their physical body. Places where they have lived are often permeated by their thoughts—just as when the fire in a stove is extinguished the heat lingers in the room for a long time after. Places and locations have their own characteristics, their strong and weak points. The origin of the strength of any location, whether it is a small town or a whole country, is a result of the composite thought of those who live there now as well as those who previously lived there. Places carry these energies and when we enter into such a space we come under their influence and we may find a change in our thinking and acting. This effect takes place unconsciously. For example if we go to the Himalayas we are exposed to the powerful influence of the thoughts of many sages, both past and present. Our thoughts tune to their energy, manifesting as a desire to deepen our spiritual practice. Our thoughts become more spiritual and holy. We rise to the level of the prevailing thoughts. If we have a relatively mediocre and weak mind and decide to move into an inactive, inert community with low-energy, our activities and our mental vibration will start to degenerate, we will have less power and inertia will set in. We will sink to the vibratory level of the community. This of course, is not the case if we have built up a strong, positive individuality of mind. We will not be affected so easily by opposing characteristics. In fact we can actually positively influence the community and can infuse new ideas and life into it. But most of us are strongly influenced by the general thought vibrations of our locality. We draw to ourselves outside thoughts corresponding to those produced by our own mind, and are influenced by those very thoughts that we have attracted. It is a case of adding fuel to the fire. Thought waves of previous residents often affect those who move into a new home. Some houses have an unpleasant and repugnant energy, others an atmosphere of calm and happiness. Places in which crimes have been committed often carry a dark atmosphere, arising from the strong thought sent forth by both criminal and victim. The atmosphere of an old church or temple is apt to produce a feeling of quiet and calm. Similarly some people have an aura of strength, peace and courage about them, while others an air of disharmony, distrust and disquiet.

The power to create, affect, modify and accomplish is all yours for the having! Expand the mind, open your heart, think big. Think bigger than you are at present, think greater than you have ever been, contemplate the seemingly impossible - that you are the fountain of great power, sweetness, joy and wisdom!

Thought is a living force with a pronounced power. Thought is always in the active and attracting mode. It acts as a magnet. It impacts the very mind that has produced it, other minds that are in a similar vibrational state, the whole mental atmosphere comprising of all minds, and it affects and molds matter.

The power of thought depends on the degree of concentration and purity, the quality of emotion and the quality of intention with which it is charged. Intention is to set a purpose that activates and releases our prana or energy. With a strong intention there is a surge of prana that accompanies the projected thought. The greater the power of concentration, purity, emotion and intention behind a thought, the greater its effect and the sooner its fructification. Let the mind develop the habit of cultivating only harmonious, higher quality thoughts and soon you will attract to yourself more auspicious conditions, ones in consonance with higher types of thought. The doors of opportunity, grace and a greater spiritual awakening will open wide for you!

Those of strong will send forth strong thoughts and consciously or unconsciously project along with them a quantity of prana or energy proportional to the force with which the thought was propelled. Such thoughts can be compared to the firing of a bullet. The impact is palpable. Well-known public speakers and orators have acquired this art of thought projection. The thoughts of those whose will is strong as well as selfless bring profound changes to the world. Similarly, thought forms sent, often unconsciously, by those whose minds are filled with selfish desires and objectives affect others negatively. Yet there is no need to fear such people; our own thoughts of love, strength and positivity act as a protective shield. It is our duty and responsibility to maintain a positive mental atmosphere. This is certainly not easily accomplished but quite possible with proper training. Thoughts of love, kindness, generosity and selflessness are like body armor, repelling even the strongest negative thought waves found in the astral atmosphere or those that are specifically aimed against us. The higher the order of thought the stronger it is.

The most important conditions for the development of a positively powerful mind are purity and truthfulness. The mind that is purified and free of negativity becomes very powerful. Whatever we concentrate on with a pure mind we quickly attract and our thoughts materialize quickly. Thoughts are powerful in proportion to their intensity, feeling and depth. Whatever idea we think of, imagine or desire consistently leads to the materialization of that idea.

Remember that thought attracts other thoughts of a similar nature. Therefore be aware and responsible and send only positive thoughts. When you want to transmit a thought, visualize a golden stream of electrical waves along with your energy. It will attract the energy and support of other thoughts of a similar nature. We send thoughts and as we do so simultaneously we attract the kind of thoughts we send. The thought of only one strong thinker overcomes the weak, purposeless thoughts of the many who send forth negative thoughts. The positive is a sure antidote to the negative.

Thoughts are closely connected with our desires. In fact desires are nothing but emotionally-charged thoughts. Our strong desire creates thought forms, which work together for the gratification of those desires, whether good or bad. Such thought forms become powerful helpers, and never sleep or tire in their work! We should never send forth a strong thought-desire unless it meets the standards of our higher mind or the highest self, or without its approval. We must always remember that in no circumstance should we ever send forth a strong thought-desire in order to injure another. Negative thoughts projected against a pure mind will rebound to the sender, stronger than before.

The nature of the mind is such that it becomes that which it intensely thinks of. Thus if you think of the negative qualities of another person, your mind will be charged with these negative qualities at least for the time being. Those who know this psychological law will never indulge in censuring others or in finding fault in the conduct of others, will see only the good in others, and will always praise others. This practice enables one to grow in concentration, Yoga and spirituality.

Swami Sivananda

Reflect when thinking of others. Whatever thought we have about others comes back to us like a boomerang. We bathe in the vibrations and the quality of thoughts sent to others. Our experience of happiness can never be independent of how we think of others. Eliminate every excuse for dwelling on others' faults. Dwelling on others' qualities creates the very same impressions in our own mind. Our mind is charged by whatever we think about. If we think of someone's negative qualities, they will slowly work their way into our own consciousness and we will soon exhibit the same qualities. It is a good spiritual discipline to contemplate and think of the good qualities of others. Such a practice benefits all.

Tune to the higher vibrations. Only those whose spiritual development is great possess the highest mental powers. Such masters are constantly sending forth thought waves of strength and help. We can easily attune ourselves to their positive thought-vibration. All we have to do is mentally call for their support, and while maintaining a peaceful and quiet state of mind, we will soon feel their beneficent influence, helping us to think better thoughts, make wiser choices, and encouraging us in solving our problems. If we have a genuine intention we will at once attract waves of strong, spiritual thoughts, which are constantly emanating from the minds of these helpers of the human race, regardless of whether they are still living in the physical body or not. Note though that this process of attuning has to be regular.

We are all creators. There are wonderful possibilities open to all of us who wish to take advantage of the storage of thought from the vast ocean of thoughts. In this 'thought-storage' there are many powerful thoughts that have emanated from the minds of the great both past and present. They include the seeds of some of the most marvellous inventions of modern science, arts and spirituality. If we can tune to them our creative work will take on a new dimension. We will find solutions to our own individual problems as well as to those of humanity. Our creativity simply increases when we understand that we are not the only creators and thinkers. We all share the same thought-storage!

Many of our highest thoughts individually and collectively have come down to us in the form of inspiration or insight from some of the world's greatest thinkers. To this we add our own thought force. The creative process of finding solutions and new avenues for humanity has come to us through the medium of many minds. Many have thought intently upon a particular subject, opening themselves up to outside thought influences, which have then hastened toward their receptive minds. The desired plan or the missing link entered into their field of consciousness, resulting in remarkable discoveries within their area of expertise. In this vast arena of thought there are many that are still lying unexpressed and are seeking an outlet. If a creative thinker has generated strong ideas with considerable force of desire but has had neither the energy nor ability to act on them or to finalize them, their thoughts will seek out—often for years—other minds as a channel of expression. They can be easily drawn to the mind of one who will translate them into action. If we are open, we can be the receiver of the highest inspiration, creativity and philosophical and scientific insight.

Our bodies are, believe it or not, fashioned by our thoughts. The mind creates the body from the material of our own thoughts. Our thoughts have etched themselves into our physiognomies, faces and voices. The body is a mirror of the entire thinking process. All thoughts are 'written' somewhere in our bodies. Scientific research has proved beyond doubt that there is a relationship between our thoughts and health. The body is an organic whole governed by an intelligence beyond our comprehension. Each cell has a tiny brain and all cells communicate between themselves in an extraordinary manner outside our conscious mind. This communication is possible because of the presence of one uniform and homogenous consciousness or intelligence. The system through which the body works is very precise. If we try to override the program, for example by eating too much or overworking or holding onto negative thoughts for too long, the body will adapt for some time but will eventually break down.

Let us see explore some simple facts about how thoughts are imprinted in our bodies.

Our face is an index of our thoughts. Every thought creates a tiny groove. Every positive and sublime thought brightens the face while a negative one leaves a 'shadow.' If we maintain positive, pure and selfless thoughts for a long time, the aura around our face will increase. And the opposite is true; if we maintain negative thoughts, the dark impressions will grow.

The tone and manner of our voice clearly indicates the degree and intensity of our thoughts, more than the actual words used. If we speak softly and sweetly, we evoke a similar response from others. If our tone is harsh, commanding, arrogant or stern, the reaction from the listener will correspond to the energy we are projecting with our voice.

The body is most sensitive to the effects of our thoughts. Thoughts of fear, doubt, anger and worry poison the very source of life within and destroy harmony and vitality, whilst thoughts of joy, cheerfulness and courage heal, soothe and rejuvenate. A strong outburst of anger produces adrenaline in the system that lingers in the body for up to three or four days causing damage to brain cells, suppressing secretion of gastric juices and inducing premature aging and death.

The wisdom of both Traditional Chinese Medicine and Ayurveda contains precious information about the relationship between the organs of the body and thoughts. In Traditional Chinese Medicine the organs are paired with the meridians that run through them.

Thoughts of patience, kindness and compassion invigorate the whole system, specifically the liver and the gall bladder. The liver is affected by irritability, anger, resentment and jealousy.

Powerful thoughts of courage, inspiration and confidence, clear perception and wisdom strengthen the kidneys and bladder, whilst loneliness, fear, hopelessness, lack of will, feeling overwhelmed and lack of self-confidence injure them.

The lungs and large intestine are organs of expansion as well as release. The lungs love freedom, integrity, true happiness, ability to let go, a sense of openness and righteousness. Many of us carry grief, shame, guilt, sadness, despair and anxiety. Such thoughts negatively affect the lungs and the large intestine.

The heart is injured by thoughts of hate, separation, restlessness, anxiety, shock and sadness. The heart can be damaged by overexcitement; heart attacks are not uncommon with a lottery win or the success of a favorite team. Positive thoughts—openness, acceptance, forgiveness, oneness, peacefulness, joy, gentle laughter and tenderness—nurture the hear; orderliness strengthens it.

The spleen, pancreas and stomach are energetically connected. Worried thoughts, obsessive thoughts, mistrust and overthinking damage the spleen and to some degree the stomach; sympathy and trust nurture the spleen. Criticism and scepticism affect the stomach and pancreas; thoughts of understanding and wisdom nurture them.

Thought is a force that can change, transform, or modify any aspect of the human body. Since our body is fashioned according to the quality of our thoughts, as we work on our thoughts and they change, the body will also change. Make it an imperative to think only in the most positive ways and cherish and cultivate only good thoughts. Do not regard negative thoughts lightly. This requires vigilance and the exercise of discrimination. Vow to keep up the highest vibratory level of thought and the body will respond to this magnificent change.

CHAPTER 4

THOUGHTS — SEEDS OF OUR FUTURE

You are the master of your destiny
You can do and undo things
If you sow a thought you will reap an action
If you sow an action you will reap a tendency
If you sow a tendency you will reap a habit
If you sow a habit you will reap your character
If you sow your character you will reap destiny
Therefore destiny is your own creation

Swami Sivananda

Thoughts are the seeds of our mental states out of which our experiences, our environment and all our material conditions are the fruits we reap.

To know that the universe is but the objectified form of thought, and at the same time, to experience the Awareness that is beyond all phenomena, is the pinnacle of all spiritual striving. To realize that all our joys and sorrows, circumstances and experiences, down to the smallest detail, are nothing but the thoughts of past and future manifested—and that yet there is Consciousness beyond it—is true knowledge.

Thoughts, just like fiber in cloth, are woven into the fabric of our destiny. The thoughts of yesterday have become our present and the thoughts of today will become our future. Whenever we maintain strong thoughts or repeated thoughts about an object they build momentum and once they reach critical mass they crystallize into actions. All actions, whether those of the mind, the senses, or our words, result from this same process. Reality is nothing but the reflection of our thoughts. The mind, just like iron, is magnetized by an object, or more precisely in the case of the mind, by its own imagining of it.

Thought is the beginning of creation. All manifestation has a thought as its cause. We are the witness of the power of our thoughts in the form of our bodies, environment, suffering and happiness. We may be tempted to think negatively but remember that the power to steer the mind in the direction of positive and constructive thoughts is in our hands. It is a matter of practice and faith.

We are perfectly free to manifest anything we want. But in order to do so thought needs to be nurtured on a very deep level. All of us must awaken to the power of thought. We live in an age in which we are becoming progressively more aware of the power of thought. We see that the power of thought can be used for good and bad purpose. The choice is clearly presented to us. Let it be courage, tolerance, beauty and wisdom that we choose.

The mind is made of impressions, thoughts, and habits. Spiritual life means building new habits, new ways of thinking, seeing, feeling and acting. By changing our habits we can also change our character. Habits originate from the thoughts and actions in the conscious mind. However, when they become established by constant repetition they sink into the depths of the unconscious mind and become our second nature. Habits become the power that controls a great deal of our active life.

Our effort is our destiny. Man determines his own destiny by his thought. He can make those things also happen which were not destined to happen. The soul of man is powerful enough. One should therefore overcome one's unfavorable destiny (the effect of one's past efforts) by greater effort in the present. There is nothing in the world which cannot be achieved by man by right sort of efforts. Destiny is simply the limitation imposed by an already exercised freedom of choice, or what is commonly called free will.

Yoga Vasishtha

That which we think of the most, that which preoccupies our mind the most becomes our destiny. Destiny is built of thoughts. Each one of us is the maker of ourselves. Other people, circumstances and factors only appear to shape our lives. What we experience has already been predetermined to a large degree by our previous choices. What we have loved in the past but which at that time caused us suffering is something that we may unconsciously or consciously dislike now. For example if I was a heavy smoker in one of my previous lives and it caused me tremendous suffering, I now may not be able to bear to be around smoking. We all experience conflict between our past and current desires.

How would we feel if we truly knew that our lives are completely shaped by our thoughts and feelings—rather than by external factors and people? Just as we build a house brick by brick; similarly every morning we must lay a foundation of powerful positive thoughts, and more importantly, pour our soulforce into them with the intention that they will manifest at that very moment. And then we must reawaken their strength throughout the day. Gradually we will start to understand that we are the architect of our destiny.

The world is nothing but a mirror of one's own self. Through the law of affinity our strengths as well as our unresolved issues find their corresponding manifestations in the world we

43

encounter daily. We attract only what we are. And we are what we think. Remember that the power of the law of affinity manifests only to some degree with the superficial thoughts of the conscious mind. But the thinking process is not limited only to this level. In order for the law of attraction to truly operate the magnetic pull has to come from the deepest layers of our being. What we truly are, deeply within, is what we will attract to ourselves. Translate your most important thoughts into your deepest beliefs—something that can happen only when we start to live our thoughts.

Our mind is omnipotent because thought is endowed with creative power. Whatever we concentrate on intensely, materializes. Nothing can ever be created but through power of the mind. Thought is the material out of which all things are made, and all matter is simply the materialization of consciousness. We have the power to create a new world in which the values can be that of love, compassion and giving. Employ pure intention, pure thought and pure action. Every foundation is first built on the level of thought, followed by action. This process requires consistency and perseverance. Choose a quality you would like to develop. Begin by visualizing that quality first, and then act in accordance with your new plan.

Suppose that on a daily basis we maintain thoughts of kindness, and we ponder over the many wonderful aspects of joy and love that the practice of kindness unfolds. Watch how it enriches others' lives and how it spreads—like the sun—its light and warmth flowing into the hearts of all. See how it alleviates the suffering we see all around us, and how it makes life more bearable and meaningful. This type of contemplation will inspire us to do many kind acts, such as to look or speak kindly, consoling and helping others. The more kind acts we do the greater the momentum and the propelling force we will create; and soon our actions will manifest as a tendency to do even more actions of the same nature. Gradually a strong habit will be formed. A habit is nothing but second nature. It strikes its root deep into the fertile soil of our mind and adds to our character.

Such will be its presence and power that our first impulse in dealing with others will be rooted in kindness. Others will talk about us as kind, who they would love to have as a friend. There are also other fruits on this wonderful tree of kindness, which we will draw to ourselves—good health, agreeable people and favorable circumstances. The destiny of those who are kind is like a soft fabric in which each fiber is made up of kindness.

Now look at anger. Let's say that we are deeply frustrated with our life and think predominantly angry thoughts. We are unable to find peace and are irritable and short-fused. Perhaps we don't actually think that anger is a sign of strength, but in our anger we may believe that it is the only way to change and move things in our life. Perhaps we feel a sense of empowerment when releasing anger in order to accomplish our goals. Gradually by dwelling on thoughts of anger we allow the seed of anger to take root, finding ourselves doing more and more actions in anger. We speak angrily, curse, shout, and even throw things around in desperation. Anger feeds anger. The more the anger, the greater its momentum, and soon it becomes not only a tendency but a strong habit and then established in our character. Our first impulse in dealing with others will now be rooted in anger. Others will look at us as an angry person, avoiding contact. It will be difficult for us to find peace of mind and to make friends. Our life will quickly fill with enemies of all kinds. We may lose our job or partner, and most importantly, our health. And we have become a magnet for more anger. We end up living in paranoia, believing that the world is only out to make us angry. The destiny of the angry is sadness and desperation.

The limit of your thought is the limit of your possibilities. Your circumstances and environments are the materialization of your thoughts. The world experience rises or falls in accordance with your thoughts. Whatever thought is cherished by you in the world will be ultimately realized.

Swami Sivananda

Thought is the means of our rise or fall in life. We are continuously shaping our reality by the quality and intensity of our thought. What we perceive as our current life has been shaped by numerous thoughts and the most powerful desires of the past. If we accept the truth that all our thoughts will eventually materialize then we must take responsibility to think our best thoughts. The beginning of each day, each week, each moment is the birth of a new life. Sow only the seeds of love and understanding, wisdom and joy—the seeds of better vision and greater hope and insight.

Spiritual economy is summarized in a few words: supply the positive and the negative will have no place. Keep vigilant and economize on your mental energy so that you think, hear, see and say only what is absolutely necessary. You will have plenty of energy. Look at thought as the means of evolution, as the means of building yourself and your destiny. Every thought has the power to materialize at some time or another. Think your best thoughts and let actions follow. There will be a struggle to reach the point where the mind is able to see only good and positive, and when the whole lake of the mind will be of a positive nature alone but Swami Sivananda tells us, *"Life is full of struggle, let us celebrate the struggle!"*

Destroy ruthlessly the fearthoughts, selfish thoughts, the hate-thoughts, lustful thoughts, and other morbid negative thoughts. These evil thoughts induce weakness, disease, disharmony, depression and despair. Cultivate positive thoughts such as mercy, courage, love and purity. The negative thoughts will die by themselves. Try this and feel your strength. Pure thoughts will infuse in you a new exalted life.

Swami Sivananda

In order to gain a greater understanding of the many types of thoughts that occur in the mind, we can divide them into groupings, making them easier to recognize and control. Here are a few common groupings.

Gloomy thoughts have a generally low vibration. They can be pessimistic, dark thoughts that involve complaining, whining, self-pity, depressing or chaotic thoughts, thoughts of hopelessness, lethargy and purposelessness.

Worry is one of the greatest enemies of life, joy and health. Worry appears to be suggestive of reasonable and constructive thinking whereas in reality it is its opposite. The moment we worry the mind becomes steeped in fear and negativity. Worry does great harm to the astral body and the mind. It causes 'inflammation' of the astral body and drains its vital force. Worrying wastes a tremendous amount of energy. Take special care that worry is kept out of the domain of your creative mind. Like a strong and vigilant guard let your awareness protect you from such thoughts. Have zero tolerance for even a single worry in your mind. Banish this terrible curse of modern living by merging your mind in the contemplation of the Divine. Sing and dance the song of joy, the song of your birthright! Since worry is such a persistent habit, different methods need to be employed daily to eradicate it—from meditation, prayer and asanas to right thought, right action and right conduct. Stamp out worry by the practice of constructive thinking, vigilant introspection, and keep your mind fully occupied while remaining positive and joyful.

Grief destroys strength, health, intellect and wisdom. Conquer grief through discrimination, enquiry and meditation on the Atman (Self).

Swami Sivananda

Many of us carry grief from what we have loved and lost. Grief is a by-product of wanting to hold onto objects, people and experiences, resisting movement with the times. It is a companion of not wanting things to change. It belongs to the realm of matter, to that of name and formant is a direct opponent of joy which is the ornament of our true Self. Let grief go. Open the doors of faith and hope wide and let the rays of the sun of your true nature come in.

Guilt is the feeling of remorse as the result of a negative action. Even though guilt is a sign that we have crossed the boundaries of righteousness and love, we have to remember that letting the feeling govern our life will only make us more depressed. Guilt changes nothing. If past mistakes are followed by a will and determination to change then we leave the past behind where it belongs and make a fresh start. The only way to overcome the painful past is by focusing on what we want to become in the future and so make best use of the present. Guilt leads to stagnation of energy; it can make us feel 'stuck' so that we stay in the same mental place for years. Life experience is a dynamic teacher. If we are willing to pay the debt incurred and move forward we are set free. We can learn the greatest lessons from our own mistakes. Let your principle be to do your best! Nature allows repair and healing. All of us must make some mistakes in the large arena of life. We are all baby souls and mistakes are part of our growth. It is due to them that we have become more cautious and sensitive. Gradually increase discrimination, devotion, non-attachment and the attitude of gratitude and prayerfulness in your heart and you will soon see the results—a life full of purpose, grace and love.

Angry and judgmental thoughts include irritability, thoughts of criticism, sarcasm, bickering and more. Anger is one of the most common and destructive delusions and afflicts our mind almost every day. It is easier to react to anger with anger; it is harder to respond with forbearance, forgiveness, tolerance or patience.

Anger may give us a tremendous sense of power, but at the same time it undermines our own happiness and that of others. Imagine what our day would look like without irritability or anger? How many moments, days, or even years have been lost in unnecessary grudges and resentments that seem to poison so many lives? Do you think that you get angry only with people? What about getting upset about the weather, or your pet, or spilling your coffee just seconds before you leave the house? Or the circumstances of your life—your partner, job? So many lost moments can be saved by the simple realization that anger can be transformed into a creative force and into wisdom.

Instinctive thoughts—thoughts of fear, fear of death or illness, anxiety, lust, deep anger, all forms of worries are very powerful and need proper management. We share many instincts with animals—survival; reproduction; avoiding injury, pain and hurt; combat; protecting country, family and possessions; curiosity; herding; impulsive likes and dislikes; assertiveness; exploitation, manipulation and lordship over others; and destructive instincts—which are frequently the driving force behind many of our actions.

Obsessive thoughts can belong to any of the groupings above, but particularly instinctive thoughts, which are fuelled by fear, anger, lust or greed. Negative thoughts and talk about others have an obsessive element in them.

Intrusive thoughts may include all sudden thoughts, obsessive thoughts, memories of old pleasures or hurts, and thoughts characterized by a general lack of focus. Such stray thoughts grab our attention without us noticing. Intrusive thoughts include making plans when we are supposed to be focused elsewhere, imaginations, little worries and distractive sounds and images. These have a tendency to appear partcularly at the time of our meditation practice. Whenever our mind is left with no focus and starts to roam intrusive thoughts fill the vacuum.

Unimportant thoughts are useless, unnecessary and untimely and are unrelated to the subject of our thinking. They are irrelevant to our work. So many of us are unaware that we can choose our thoughts and instead are caught up in a whirlpool of irrelevance. Thoughts related to a past conversation, checking email, the news, social media or the weather frequently, or dwelling on gossip are all examples of this.

Worldly thoughts are thoughts focused on the ever-changing values of the world, and the perception of this world as the true reality. These thoughts may include thinking about money, business, looks, fashion, cars, identification with the values presented by society, thinking that others are happier than oneself, or thinking about pleasures.

Unwholesome thoughts include lustful, vulgar, malicious thoughts, dark and perverse thoughts, thoughts based on greed, lust, anger and selfishness. As with all negative thoughts these originate from the karmic seeds resulting from negative actions we have committed either in the past or in this lifetime.

Habitual thoughts are those which are maintained by habit only. We move in a narrow circle of likes and dislikes and use expressions such as, 'I always do this,' or 'I tend to like this or that,' or

'I never do such a thing.' The mind becomes set in its ways and we feel consciously or unconsciously frozen. Habitual thoughts involve maintaining the same thoughts for example in relation to food, body, dress, people, relationships, job. We simply stagnate in the mire of our opinions. We need to exercise our mind and be fresh and flexible in the way we think about the things we encounter daily.

Use your mind as a filter; watch and do not allow any useless thought to enter. Screen out all useless thoughts. Make no compromise with negative thoughts—they can be very convincing at times. They have been robbing you of your strength for so long. Now is the time for change. Your beautiful Self within urges you to abandon and transcend these thoughts. The first rule of the game: keep the focus on the positive and the negative will die by itself. What a joy to feel a new life flowing through us in the form of positivity, hope, love and faith!

Positive thoughts can be categorized into two groupings. The many types of negative thoughts mentioned above can be compared to the weeds in the garden of our mind, whilst our positive thoughts are the beautiful flowers. Positive thoughts are our true wealth and we must try our best to cultivate them consciously.

Inspirational thoughts When inspirational thoughts appear, be ready to act on them! As our mind senses the refreshing breeze of inspirational thought, we feel as if soft powerful currents filled with life have entered us; we feel elated and light as if gently borne into the air. Lightness, freshness and joy accompany these thoughts. We become aware of enormous possibilities and are filled with hope, enthusiasm, love and feelings of empowerment. At times these thoughts may come as a flash, illuminating the whole field of our mind and warming our heart. If we follow them and live them both outwardly and inwardly we will sense the mission which we have been given. Inspirational thoughts adorn the minds of great artists, scientists, researchers, philosophers, selfless workers and all inspired loving and spiritual people. Many inspirational thoughts can be gathered from spiritual sources, scriptures, talks and books written by enlightened masters. Take special care to garner them, nurture them, keep them close to your heart and live them! Write inspirational sayings in your notebook or diary and reflect frequently upon their meanings and message. Memorize them and repeat them frequently during the day. There are many books and scriptures that contain the most precious and illuminating essence. Verses from the Bible, the Dhammapada, the Bhagavad Gita, the Upanishads and innumerable others contain this essence of inspiration.

Illuminating thoughts provide insight and increase our knowledge and discriminative power. These thoughts can be also inspirational; both types have much in common. Reflection on the preciousness of one's life, on the meaning of love and virtue, on the importance of wisdom and similar thoughts come under this grouping.

Take time to dwell on the meanings of inspirational and illuminating thoughts and let their deep message bring you back home to the purpose of your life.

Wholesome or virtuous thoughts are the seeds or the expressions of virtues such as kindness, forgiveness, gentleness, generosity, patience and selflessness. They open our heart and widen our consciousness bringing joy into our being. These are the most important thoughts, to be cultivated by all. They purge and purify negative thoughts and tendencies that may have taken hold of our minds and at the same time enrich our minds with nobility and direction, leading us eventually to the knowledge of our true nature.

CHAPTER 5

LIVING WITH PURPOSE

The life of man is an indication of what is beyond him and what determines the course of his thoughts, feelings and actions. The wider life is invisible, and the visible is a shadow cast by the invisible which is the real. The shadow gives an idea of the substance, and one can pursue the path to the true substance by the perception of the shadow. Human existence, by the fact of its limitations, wants and various forms of restlessness, discontent and sorrow, points to a higher desired end, incomprehensible though the nature of this end being.

Swami Sivananda

Physical life in matter is nothing but a sign and a revelation of the Supreme Spirit or Consciousness. The visible is a symbol of the invisible. The very struggle against limitation is nothing but an unconscious striving to reach the Unlimited. Recognize the presence of the unchangeable within the changeable, (i.e. in the forms and names), and you will discover the key to immortality.

Rediscovering our purpose also means taking responsibility for our life—commonly known as maturity. When we are awakened to the numerous possibilities that lie ahead of us, when we start to feel our own strength by making the right choices and thinking the best thoughts, we cease to depend on others for our happiness. We realize that true power lies within us only and that no one else can give it to us. No one can discipline the mind for us. Once this realization dawns we stop using our circumstances as an excuse for not wanting to grow. In reality the only thing that matters is our effort. If other people and conditions seem to control our lives it is only because we do not exercise our will and our creative power of thought sufficiently. Take your life into your hands and you will know the true meaning of freedom. Creative power of thought is the privilege of every mind. Our own efforts guided by our aspiration are the very fiber of our destiny. Do not let the mind become dissipated by cherishing weak thoughts. The untrained mind can manifest neither strength nor depth of insight. Anything that is thought of with intensity will become reality sooner or later, in accordance with one's effort.

It is unfortunate that most of us do not believe enough in our own power of thought and so live in a bondage of our own creation. Yet it is never too late to reverse this process and use our thoughts in the direction of freedom and plenty. Right aspiration with persistence is the secret to changing what appears to be impossible—our destiny. Work incessantly for your freedom and work for it every moment of the day. Never let yourself tire of working on your mind as, indeed, there is nothing more powerful than the mind. One who has conquered the mind has conquered all the forces of nature and death itself.

The vast majority of us have no definite aim in life. We drift. We have energy and we have intellectual, artistic, physical or other capabilities, and yet we have no clear-cut program in life. If an ideal is alive we can develop a gigantic will. Understand clearly the purpose of life and then design a plan that is aligned with its achievement. Ever live up to your ideal.

Have you ever contemplated what it really means to be human? What is so special about entering into the human body and living life as a human being? To be born means to be born with countless possibilities. To live is to discover our infinite potential and we have a whole lifetime to experiment and improve upon it. Is there anything that a human being cannot attain? Everything is potentially within our reach and our realization. We only have to employ the correct laws of thought. Human life is indeed very precious! To be human is to discover what being alive really means—to unlock the hidden wealth of the Divine within.

How few of us value life! Our mind is often lost in the mirage of temptation and wrong pursuit, wandering without purpose amongst empty shadows and phantoms of entertainment. Our days and hours are wasted in useless pursuits. It is not until we are stricken by adversity that we start to open our eyes to life. Tell the mind, "It's time to wake up, O mind! There is a glorious future waiting for you!"

There is a plan and purpose for each one of us within creation, whether we are conscious of it or not. The purpose of life is to rise above, to transcend the limitations of life. All sense of inadequacy and smallness, of imperfection and limitation is to be destroyed. Our life is meant to be a spring of strength and joy and it is for us to discover this within ourselves. It may seem as if we are overwhelmed by problems and challenges; we may feel stripped of choices and yet, something in us, our higher purpose, keeps us striving!

For the power of thought to manifest and for our life to be well-lived we need an orientation and purpose. Ask yourself these questions:

- Is there a purpose to my life higher than that of family, work, education, friends and relationships?

- Does a higher purpose exist for all beings? Is such a purpose a common destination of all beings or does it belong only to the realm of individual life?

And more practically:

- If I had more free time how would I use it?

- If I had plenty of wealth and resources how would I use them?

- When a person dear to me has passed on what are my thoughts? Does it make me consider changing the way I live?

- If I had only one year to live how would I like to spend that time?

There is a central purpose of life, the ultimate spiritual purpose—Self-Realization, Self-knowledge or Enlightenment. The central purpose of life directs and centralizes our thoughts and desires. We may call these aspirations and they are linked to and lead us to the realization of the ultimate purpose. Just as all rivers flow toward one common ocean, so also all beings gravitate and move toward one common source which we may call God, the Divine, Happiness, Pure Love or Truth.

The highest purpose in life is spiritual in nature, and it is the realization of the one common principle, one common life, one Consciousness behind all forms and names, behind all appearances. That spiritual principle or reality is hidden like butter in milk—it has to be 'churned' by our contemplation, meditation and selfless life. The spiritual purpose of life obliges us to contribute to the wellbeing and happiness of others, in short, to become selfless. It is only selfless living that can embody the highest purpose of life and yield the greatest happiness. Most of us think that fulfillment of our personal desires is the primary objective of our lives. However, this narrow and exclusive focus necessarily limits our energies and powers. When we widen the scope of our actions to include others, our vision expands and we naturally find a greater influx of energy, we feel the support of many people and higher beings. The closer we come to understanding what the purpose of our life is, the better organized our energies, the more positive our thoughts, and the more meaningful our life.

We must learn to recognize that there is only one main purpose in life. Our aspirations are secondary to it, but must contribute to the realization of the primary purpose. Our daily activities must be connected to the main purpose. If we don't think this way there will be a 'disconnect' between what we are aspiring for and what we are actually doing. For this reason it is important that the means and the purpose are in accord where the means are the supporting agents of the realization of the purpose.

Suppose we aspire to achieve a peaceful state of mind. Then all our actions are to reflect and carry the essence of the state of peace—the absence of agitation, commotion and chaos, and the presence of gentleness and compassion. The manner in which we relate to ourselves and treat others are to reflect our wish to achieve peace. The peaceful actions we perform will be the means to achieve peace. Suppose we talk about peace, hope to achieve peace, dream about it, but in our words there are still judgments that hurt, or we lack sensitivity with regard to others' needs, or we exhibit the desire to control them. Then we still have to make that true walk of a peacemaker and will need to correct all the actions that are opposed to and which are taking us away from the objective–that of peace.

The next factor to look at is how efficiently we manage our time. Our lives are dominated by the desire for physical, emotional and intellectual pleasures; how we fritter away time on that which is transitory! We have lives that are characterized by the absence of higher ideals. As you go about your day, protect your mind from these two pitfalls: that of letting your mind become scattered or dissipated and that of entertaining negative and powerless thoughts—they are often interconnected. Our management of time shows us what we prioritize in life. Even though we live in times where we feel stretched to the limit by the demands of work, family and social lives, still we find the time for what we consider important and what we love. The question behind our priorities is related to the nature of our love or our faith, one and the same in this instance. We will always find time for the things we love. The truth is that the time for doing what we love is created by our own mind, by the heart's deepest longing for a particular ob activity or experience. If we find ourselves making excuses for missing a yoga class or meditation, it is because we believe it is not so important, our heart is not fully engaged. We could say we have no love for it. Suppose for example we have to get up at 5am to travel to our favorite island for a vacation—no problem! But if we are asked to rise at the same time to meditate—much too early! It takes time to learn to deeply appreciate activities like this. To put time into endeavors that benefit us may not be easy or may not even seem profitable in the beginning, but with a little discipline and willpower, we slowly come to value the experience.

There are two ways to create or open up more time for something we would like to do. One is to increase our interest in the activity, for example, by reading more about it, attending a talk, watching a video or talking about it to friends. As our interest increases we start to make more time for it. Another is to be vigilant in utilizing whatever little time we do have in its pursuit.

Since there is an incredible potential for us to be distracted at any given moment of the day, it is important that we build our day's foundation in the early morning by doing a few yoga asanas or other forms of exercise, and by meditating. This is essential. If we leave these practices for later in the day, we find there is no time or inclination left to do them. All wisdom is born at dawn. We find that the challenges the day brings will be considerably lessened if we simply stay grounded in the greater awareness of our Being, created by a spiritual routine.

Even a little venture into the mind soon tells us that we have both good and bad 'raw' material to work with. Now we need to engage our creativity in working with it. We probably never thought that working with our weaknesses would be a creative and enlightening process. The only true victory is victory over our mind; it is only the conquest over our mind that constitutes real happiness and it is the greatest treasure. Only when we are able to understand and manage our own mind can we effectively help others find their happiness too. As we work with our weaknesses and strengths it is important to know that human beings do not differ so much in kind as in measure. Some may have more of one quality than another. Great masters and sages have positive qualities developed to such a large extent that we could say that they possess them in absolute measure. These qualities fully permeate their personality. The question is how can we bring a positive quality to a higher level and ultimately the absolute level where we feel that this quality has become part of our whole nature, always there, in everything we do? We who are still making baby steps in becoming stronger and wiser have positive qualities in a smaller, relative measure. We can look at life as a journey in which we are to develop our strengths and qualities from the relative (where we stand now) to the absolute measure of a sage. We intend to give voice and expression to the absolute values within us.

Ask yourself daily, "What is the purpose of my life, why was I born?" If you ask this question with deep intention you will soon reawaken your distant memory-like connection with the Supreme, the Divine within, the only Reality. It is that memory that moves us on to search for it and to find it. Even just for a few minutes daily, stop everything that you are doing and just rest in that Being. Soon you will know what it means to let go of striving, wanting and acting. You are simply beautiful, real and free.

For both mental and physical training, we have to work according to a plan. Control over the mind is not an inborn quality possessed by all. We have been deluded so many times by the promises of 'tomorrow'. Life is only lived in the present. Every victory however tiny can only be accomplished in the most immediate present. Make daily resolves to become a genuine and deeply spiritual person. Failures don't count for those who make such resolves. Glory to all struggling aspirants! Train your mind to be hopeful, confident, courageous and determined. As we keep our will and focus trained tenaciously on our purpose, we will attract from the thought world elements and powers favorable to that purpose.

EXERCISE
CONTEMPLATION ON THE PURPOSE OF LIFE

Spend a few minutes daily contemplating your purpose of life and how your actions are linked to its realization. Clarify your understanding of it. Sit with your eyes closed and after taking a few deep and soft breaths, bring your awareness to the question of your purpose.

- What do I think is the reason I was born?

- Am I aware how precious this human life is?

- Do I maintain respect for my ability to realize my potential?

- How deeply am I aware of my purpose?

- Am I able to state my purpose in unambiguous terms?

- How clear is the process of accomplishing my purpose?

- What is the level of my integrity? Do my actions support my purpose?

- In what actions do I generally stray away from my purpose?

- What are the reasons behind my purpose?

Now state your purpose in clear language, three times with deep feeling and with the intention that you will come closer to its realization.

My purpose is.......... and from now onwards, I will connect all my actions to my purpose!

CHAPTER 6

CHOOSING AN IDEAL

Have an ideal. You may realize it this moment or after ten years with faltering steps. It does not matter much. Endeavor your level best to live up to your ideal. Your whole energy, nerve-force and will must all be put in the realization of the ideal.

Swami Sivananda

Spiritual life is the life of perpetual striving; it is the life of incessant inner transformation. There arises in it a necessity for practical idealism. Ideals are meant to be lived. "An ounce of practice is better than tons of theory," states Swami Sivananda. Many of us have great ideas and even ideals but we don't know how to translate them into a living reality. We will achieve only that which we practice and on which we deeply contemplate. Superficial thinking won't do. It will bear no strength to produce the experience. It is a matter of complete immersion into what we want to become. By leading a spiritual life we set up a structure in which we can have the experience of that which we intensely practice and on that which we contemplate. We all want to embody something grander than we are presently. There is an inherent urge within us to move towards higher and higher forms of realization of our own ideals.

That which makes genuine spiritual teachers so special is they are living examples of what was initially only their theoretical knowledge or belief. They worked hard to gain experience, which they now share with others. When they teach, what they say moves us; their knowledge and their power of conviction enchant us because they embody a certain quality—they 'walk their talk'. This is what we call charisma or magnetism. It simply means that their experience has been etched deeply into their life and has become the very essence of who they are as teachers. They have a pervasive aura around them through which they influence all who come near. This is the power of genuine spiritual experience. Many of these qualities are the result of experiences from previous lifetimes. Remember that experience is our real teacher and that it is a supremely valuable asset. We may be inspired by people or books, but we ourselves must practice.

Just as in our daily life when we want to succeed we are proactive, so success and mastery over our mind is a matter of being practical, always striving. Just as a building needs a firm foundation so too does our spiritual life. What we think is what we become. Our growth depends largely on having an ideal and our ability to give form to it or manifest it in daily life. To work for an ideal is to put in the effort of our whole being, not only of some small aspect, to embody a particular quality or to attain success in some aspect of our practice. To live with an ideal in our heart is to be forever young.

The greatest impelling force in life is to have an ideal. It is our ideals that shape our thoughts, words and actions. By choosing an ideal we set the bar high, a standard of certain realization and achievement. The greater our ideal the greater the transformational power it exerts upon us.

An ideal is a principle or a value that we actively pursue with heart and mind. The boundaries of a spiritual ideal are large and so there is always scope for improvement. It is to have a vision, to be able to project ourselves into the future, and to see ourselves as if we have already achieved our goal. Vision keeps us in a certain state of expectancy and belief that we will bring the ideal to realization. Life can be compared to a block of stone that the sculptor is about to chisel. We are the artist, and the means of shaping an amorphous piece of stone—our life—into a form, is the effect of our thoughts and ideals.

Think of the time when you were a child dreaming about becoming a great musician, a carpenter, an artist, a sportsman or woman, a pilot or a yogi. The development of ideals began when we were children. Each one of us has had someone whom we admired and who inspired us by their conduct, their ability, grace or knowledge, so much so that we wanted to become just like them! We saw ourselves in that person; we saw our own potential in them, and we felt blissful just thinking that one day we would be like them. They were the symbol of the revelation of our own future greatness. In that process of unfolding within us, what we saw in the living examples of those great personalities inspired us to strive and extend beyond who we were then in order to become our future selves.

Can you remember the thrill, the energy you felt, the seemingly infinite exuberance, the excitement, the inspiration that kept your heart beating in joy moment by moment for days on end, as you were continually hoping to embody the same level of skill or knowledge possessed by the one you looked up to? Well, never stop being a child, ever. There are many us who have abandoned this 'childhood'; our inspiration has dried up. The state of being young, always young; is the most precious quality indeed of all great beings. To have an ideal that never tires is nothing but the assertion of the everyouthful spirit within. To live up to an ideal is to live in the state of continuous renewal and inspiration. Such youthfulness is precisely the condition of being nurtured ceaselessly by new ideals and working towards their fulfillment, uncovering the infinite possibilities that life carries.

Each one of us follows our ideal. We cannot help but follow it. Life is pervaded by it just as a cloth is permeated by color. And just as one cannot make a distinction between the cloth and its color, so also our life cannot be understood or lived outside the ideals that pervade it. By simply observing others' actions and listening to their words we can gauge the ideal that inspires them. It is only when we have an ideal that there is an opportunity for great transformation. Our nature is complacent and mechanical, unyielding to any transformative process, unless we are fired up by love, faith and enthusiasm to realize something that is greater than our present self.

Even though an ideal and a purpose may look alike, there is a difference. An ideal is a transformative tool of our life; the birth of an ideal is impelled by a psychic force from within, by a desire for us to grow into something larger than we are now. It is an instrument to attain a certain level of perfection. Purpose is more like the final goal, or simply, a concretized form, a fulfillment, or a manifestation of the ideal or group of ideals. An ideal has no visible boundaries and within it there are levels of fulfillment. Spiritual ideals resemble goals although they are not as limited. Spiritual ideals outlive goals. They represent deep transformational processes. The ideals may even seem unachievable but that is irrelevant. Do your best to approximate them. Regardless of whether we embody the ideal, we have to live up to it as if the ideal has already manifested in our lives.

Think positively. You grow into the likeness of the thought-picture which you hold on to with sincerity and persistence. Contemplate upon your ideal into which you wish to grow. This forms part of daily spiritual life.

Swami Sivananda

The importance of spiritual aspirants to have an ideal must not be underestimated. It is a beacon light, a tool of transformation of our character. When we have a plan, we are powered from within by an invisible source of energy; the whole of our subconscious mind makes itself at our disposal to help us. We must choose ideals and precise objectives in our lives in order to avoid becoming distracted. Distraction wastes a tremendous amount of energy and potential.

There are so many advantages to having ideals. The deepest thoughts, when fostered in our heart, gradually become manifested as reality. In addition, they are vast sources of inspiration urging us to find new avenues to realization. When we live for an ideal it expands our limitations. If we had no ideals we would never strive to achieve. It is this spirit that makes the difference between a mediocre human being or a spiritual hero in the battlefield of life.

In difficult times it is the presence of our ideals that keeps us going. It is only when our minds and hearts are inspired and animated by them that we truly live. At first, our starting point may seem far away from where we would like to finish. No matter! The pursuit of the ideal will gradually and systematically remove all obstacles, flaws and imperfections. Keep the goal constantly in your mind. Never worry about how long it will take to achieve.

Life is perfected through ideals which like beacons of light guide us towards the highest. Striving to realize our ideal transforms the heart, awakens faith and enlivens. The time it takes to realize it is immaterial. So start today! Begin by creating an ethical ideal such as kindness, a health ideal such as eating well, or regularity in asana practice, and then move on to higher ones. Keep a record of them in your diary and see the magic of becoming a self-made person! Perhaps you would like to develop truthfulness, gratitude, fearlessness, becoming an embodiment of a great virtue. Or maybe you would like to work for the removal of poverty and injustice in society, or for the uplifting of humanity, and most importantly for your own spiritual development. Spiritual ideals vary but what they have in common is that they must integrate with our lives and be practiced daily. Let the ideal be something that is natural to you. Do not imitate another's ideal. Contemplate the lives of the great who inspire you, discover an ideal that stimulates you the most and banish the word 'impossible' from your vocabulary for ever!

To find your ideal, reflect on your replies to the questions below. In addition you may feel inspired to add some of your own or some reflections. Write them down!

- What activity or role in life expresses the best representation of who you are?

- What ethical and spiritual principles are the most dominant in your thoughts?

- What do you envision to be your greatest achievement in life?

- What do you think you can do to help the world?

Let your mind move into the future. Your future is created by the thoughts of today! Let these thoughts slowly solidify into ideals and let them find their expression in all your actions. If we are able to sustain the vision of our ideal clearly we will attain it in no time. Do not allow it to be distorted by any negative suggestions or thoughts whatsoever. As we consistently express the new ideal, our character and our actions are deeply influenced, and we are greatly enriched.

Constantly affirm your ideal; imagine that what you envision for yourself has already become reality.

Repeat these affirmations daily:

I will live in my ideal now.
I will manifest my ideal now.
I will be my ideal now.
And all that tempts me from my ideal I will not listen to.
I will listen to the voice of my ideal!

James Allen

EXERCISE
ESTABLISHING IDEALS—MENTAL STOCKTAKING EXERCISE

Mentally go back in your life and take stock of your experiences and expectations by writing them down in sets of fives.

Five Strengths

- What are the five best qualities you think you have?

- What five strategies will enhance these good qualities?

- Make the first step today.

Five Challenges

- What are the five biggest challenges you think you have?

- What five steps will help you overcome them?

- Make the first step today.

Five Weaknesses

- What are five main weaknesses you think you have?

- What five strategies will help you overcome them?
- Make the first step today.

Five Ideals

- What are your five highest ideals?
- What five steps are you taking to fulfill them?
- Make the first step today.

Five Greatest Fears

- What are your five greatest fears?
- What five steps will help you overcome them?
- Make the first step today.

Five Greatest Hopes

- What are your five greatest hopes?
- What five steps will help you achieve them?
- Make the first step today.

CHAPTER 7

THE ART OF SELF-TRANSFORMATION

There is no higher power than the right action in the present.

Yoga Vasishta

The incomprehensible nature of the mind and its secrets elude even those who have spent a great deal of their lives studying it. It is in its nature unsteady. Just like a monkey that jumps from one branch to another, the mind hops about from thought to thought, changing its focus from a sense experience at one moment to a fantasy at another. This oscillation or restlessness of the mind makes us feel alive. It is caused by the presence of impressions (*samskaras*) and subconscious desires (*vasanas*). We often feel that if we could only fulfill our desires then we would find some tranquility. But fulfillment of desires does not resolve the problem; it only temporarily arrests the mind's wanderings. Actually the fulfillment of desires further increases the agitation and cravings. It is in the stillness of our Awareness that the mind can find complete peace.

The oscillation of the mind makes it unpredictable and is due to the action of the subtle forces within the mind called *gunas*: *tamas*, *rajas* and *sattva*. *Tamas* is the energy behind the psychological states of unawareness, inertia and lethargy. *Rajas* is associated with impulses predominantly of a selfish nature. *Sattva* is our spiritual jewel; it is the manifestation of the best qualities in a human being. The increase of sattva is the very objective of spiritual practice. Due to the constant transformation of the gunas, our moods change quickly and easily. We cannot tell from one moment to the next whether the mind will be happy or sad. When we are in a good mood we think it will last for ever, but soon we realize we cannot maintain it.

The mind has a great power of imitation. It imitates good or bad; it takes in suggestions and is easily influenced. It has two distinct aspects: imaginative and discriminative, often referred to as the lower and higher mind respectively.

The lower mind is impulsive, instinctive, and overly-emotional gripped as it were by imagination. Through this function the mind has a tendency to exaggerate experiences and generalize the specific, making our perception less accurate or plainly wrong. For example, when we observe anger in another person, we tend to exaggerate its presence, whereas the existence of the same emotion in our own mind seems so much less significant. The discriminative mind, the higher principle in us, is the one that strives for harmony and balance. This part of the mind is in tune with the deeper truth within ourselves. It is due to the power of discrimination that the mind becomes a wonderful and powerful tool in freeing us from the illusions of life. It is the instrument of the mind which examines whether our cognitive processes and our emotional and mental states are correct, arriving at the truth about the condition of the mind and giving the necessary steps required to improve it.

Mana eva manushyaanaam kaaranam bandha-mokshayoh—
Mind alone is the cause of one's bondage or liberation.

Manusmrti

In all our challenges as well as potentialities we are the creators of our strength and weakness. Every moment in life is a gift that is given to us to understand and master our thought processes. It is the very reason we are born. Driven by ignorance of our true nature and our vast potential we allow thoughts to rule our life. However once we are aware of the possibility of transforming the way we think, we are released to strive to think only constructively and positively.

Depending on how we use the mind, we can consider it as either our best friend or worst enemy. Ultimately there is no such thing as external friend or enemy; one's greatest friend and one's greatest enemy is indeed oneself. The task is to discern the voice of the higher mind. It is this voice that we should obey. Let us say that we want to wake in the morning at 5am and we succeed two days in a row. On the third day we may hear two opposing voices, one says, "Let's get up to meditate; it feels good to meditate." The other tells us, "If you get up now, you will feel tired for the rest of the day." If our mind is ruled by the lower nature, it is the 'little' self—the one associated with the body and mind, personal feelings and ambitions—that we wish to nurture and in this case we will stay in bed! The nature of the higher self, on the contrary, is characterized by the central, unitary principle which sustains all life and which links itself with others in a bond of fellowship, in the spirit of harmony and mutual help. Both the higher and lower mind have to be known through self-analysis and self-observation.

The characteristic longing of the higher self is to spread itself among others through selfless service and spiritual love, to find its ideals of truth and righteousness fulfilled in the process of its longing.

Swami Sivananda

The process of the unfoldment of the higher mind begins with the cultivation of our purest and best thoughts. Resistance and opaqueness in nature and the mind are tamasic. A mind full of tamas is like a pond which is muddy and turbid, making it hard to see the bottom. The restlessness of the mind is rajassic. The pure light that the mind becomes by thinking pure thoughts is sattvic, turning the mind into its own guide filled with love, peace, discrimination and intuitive knowledge. The process of making the mind pure is like refining gold. The same mind which has been the problem eventually becomes the solution when the higher mind gets its voice and guidance heard.

Spiritual life implies living in greater awareness, living in the moment, not letting our mind be caught in the thoughts of the past or future. The aim simply is to develop and increase our awareness. Spiritual work needs a structure and a plan. It consists of utilizing our thoughts including our negative tendencies and qualities for the fulfillment of a grand ideal of life. We are committing to breaking free from the illusion of limitations and to transcending them. Naturally this requires much training.

You must be guided by a definite principle. You must have a program for the whole life. You must know what you are and what you want to become. You must work up for the attainment of the desired goal with zeal, courage and sincerity of purpose.

Swami Sivananda

Many people are lost in the past; thinking of it with excitement and joy, or in sadness, seeing it as a source of their troubles. Likewise, the future—unknown—has nothing we can hold onto. Let your thoughts be fresh; align your thoughts and your deepest longings with your purpose. Use the finest thoughts at your disposal for attracting the most favorable circumstances and the right people. It is a matter first of conviction and then of practice. Ask yourself frequently, "What is the most fitting way to think of this particular experience, person or a situation?" Refine your thoughts and soon you will find that your character has been refined too. Self-empowerment is the key to the great achievement of self-mastery. It is the most important task ahead of you; it carries on its wings hope and determination and it creates opportunities out of every experience.

Remember that we are born with choices and even if at times these choices appear weak nevertheless they are still choices. Live your best.

How do **you** live each day? Somehow we believe that our mental world will organize itself without any plan, practice or analysis. This is wrong! We will be disappointed in the end. Mental training requires a steady and organized routine. It is essential to *live* the twenty-four hours of your day. In addition to the regular list of tasks to be done create a spiritual 'to-do list' that outlines practices that you can engage in as you move through the day. This can include some simple exercises of breathing, concentration, practice of virtues and memorizations and the frame of mind we are to maintain—but rarely pay much attention to—when we carry out basic activities such as walking, cleaning, cooking and talking. If we define spirituality as living in higher awareness then by approaching even the simplest actions as if they were our yoga practice or meditation even ordinary activities will become extraordinary, or spiritual in nature.

The beginnings of a new life are in the world of ideas or thought. We must build from the inside out. If the foundation is well-established, the building will be strong. If we nurture a particular thought each day it will eventually take root in our mind, and feelings and desires will form around it just like the molecules around a nucleus. It is the strength of feeling that in reality leads to actions. Transformation can only occur when thoughts are backed by feelings and are not simply mechanical and lifeless.

Often in our eagerness to improve our lives we tend to want to take a big leap and to insist on immediate transformation. We ignore the years of conditioning that have gone into making us who we are now. This is a typical problem for those of us who make New Year Resolutions; we do so without realizing that the changes we want to see in our lives are often unrealistic. The solution lies in the wisdom of knowing that we create our life in fragments of thoughts, feelings and actions. At any given moment our life is nothing but a conglomerate of all our actions—mental or physical. Each moment is the result of everything ever done before it. Do not make sudden changes; make them gradually. Be cautious and gentle with the mind. The mind is an energy powerful beyond our imagination. Any insistence on quick change will simply backfire and you will succumb to old habits. If you are new to an activity, and you want to do it every day, whether it is waking up early, a diet, or starting up a new meditation practice, introduce it gradually and systematically. Moving at a greater speed in life, or making bigger and faster changes than your system is accustomed to will bring bigger and faster reactions of resistance from nature. If you want to get up at 5am but you have been getting up at 8am, it might be better to start getting up at 7am or even 7:30am for at least a couple of weeks before you switch to 5am. *Natura non facil saltum*—nature never moves by leaps. Nature prefers evolution to revolution. It works in seasons. It also knows the best time for sowing the seeds of new actions and habits. The mind is part of nature and needs to conform to her laws. This does not mean that we cannot change our nature. It is just that change takes time and to instill just one habit requires regularity, skill and patience. More importantly, nature allows us to work in small increments of effort, change, love and will, one at a time. Therefore, the process needs to begin NOW! Postponement is equal to not trying. We don't initiate change tomorrow, but at this very moment. We need to disregard our failures, and focus strictly on what we can do NOW! In each of our minds lie the memories of past mistakes, but at the same time, deep within our hearts are the possibilities and hopes of a greater future and new achievements. We are all saints in the making.

Imbue your efforts with only positivity and breathe new life into them in the form of fresh, favorable beginnings. Take this as your life-motto: One step, one change at a time, however small, but well done. Learn to live all your moments with purpose, one minute at a time, making a new, positive effort one at a time. Your life will become a life well-lived. Just as tiny drops of rain form a powerful river so will your life, created through single actions of constantly-renewed effort, become an outpouring of good will, love and mighty purpose.

Let your growth be gradual by adding thought to thought, effort to effort, deed to deed. This is indeed a way to acquiring a great power. It is this that many of us do not understand. And because we no longer know the meaning of gradual growth, we give up on ourselves quickly. We also give up on others if we see that they are not changing quickly enough. We want to already be 'there'. We live in an society of instant gratification. Every process of growth and evolution is compressed and vitiated in modern times; we simply seem to have no time, and as a result, no patience. It is only in being tenacious, committed, firm, steady, patient and kind that transformation will take place.

Whatever is done frequently becomes constant—this is the principle by which all habits develop. Any action which is repeated leaves an impression in the mind and either a new impression is formed or existing impressions reinforced. Let us say that we want to develop patience. We simply vow to do as many patient actions as possible. And each time we make a conscious effort to develop patience, the quality is etched more and more deeply into the mind. This principle sounds the bell of hope and encouragement. If you do not yet see yourself where you would like to be, don't lose hope. You are bound to succeed.

Awaken your awareness and bring your mind into the present moment! So many of us are asleep! We are sleepwalkers. We are asleep to life within. We do not pay attention to our bodies, emotions, thoughts, other people and our spiritual needs and as a result we are surprised by what life brings to us. Ask yourself, "How frequently does my mind take a 'vacation'? Where does it wander?" and, "Why is it that I can think all day long yet am seldom aware of what I am thinking?!" Have you noticed that most of your thoughts slip past the eye of awareness? So many times we say, "My mind was elsewhere!" or, "I was spaced out!" How often are we caught up in absent-mindedness? Our thinking for the most part is not conscious. You will be astonished at how seldom you are aware of your mental processes. Adding more awareness to our thoughts and actions is to begin to live an authentic and rich inner and outer life.

The qualities of self-awareness and discrimination are the greatest adornments of human nature. To be aware is to discern a thought, or a mental state, an object—something that is distinct from our nature—in consecutive moments of time. What we are aware of stands outside of the awareness, and it is never of the same nature as the Consciousness that is aware. We become aware of our continually changing thoughts, but the real Self within is always aware, or more correctly, the Awareness itself does not change. The presence of Awareness within us creates the constancy or stability in perception, or the stability in knowing oneself as one unchanging observer—we do not experience the interruption of who we are.

To know that we must learn to dissociate from our thoughts is the most important discovery in life that we can make and it is the fundamental step that we must take in our quest for spiritual growth. It is the beginning of the conquest of the mind, of breaking the cycle of births and deaths (samsara). There is no happiness, no peace, no spiritual experience, unless we are able to detach from our endless stream of thoughts. All paths and all practices begin with the simple ability to be aware. The mechanistic quality of the mind is one of main reasons why we are the victims of our negative thoughts. The mind comes under the influence of what we might call the gravitational pull of the subconscious and is immersed in the countless impressions of our past experience. These impressions continually resurface, quietly slipping into the mind at times when we are not concentrating. They take their seat in the mind and make our awareness dissipate. We become lost in our thoughts—commonly known as daydreaming! Never allow any inner event or thought to appear in your mind without becoming fully aware of it. This is a truly stupendous task and the mastery of it makes the foundation for all mental and spiritual work.

When you feel a pebble in your shoe you stop to empty the shoe. In the same manner check as often as you can for any negative 'thought-pebbles' that might be in your mental space. Notice what thought has arrested your awareness, your attention. Mentally say, "This particular thought has arrested my awareness; it has caught my attention." Then at once decide to stop it and redirect your attention to either your breath, a mantra or you can simply witness it and it will disappear. This practice is more efficient in the case of less powerful negative thoughts. Unless you are able to do this exercise well, your spiritual transformation will be slow.

To be aware is to be awake and anew. Life is a flow. Just as a river that may appear unchanging actually always has new water always flowing in it, so also must we renew ourselves continuously. In the river of life nothing retains a permanent form nor ever remains the same. Life must always feel fresh and new. Each day brings us something that was not there the day before. Stay in the flow! Commit to seeing things in a new way. It is when we see objects, people and events with the same eyes, in the same mental state, that we don't see them any more. We see only the crystallized forms of our memories of them. And we lose the excitement of their presence; we stop learning about them. Apply this to your yoga practice, meditation, your friends, partner, work, any situation. Practice seeing things with a new eye. Imagine you are doing or seeing those things for the very first time.

A strong and positive mind comes when we organize and integrate all our mental activities and processes. This is very important. To think with integrity is to live with integrity. The word integrity simply means to harmonize or combine units into a whole. Integration takes place in different ways and on different levels. For example when we do what we envision can be considered as one level of integration. To speak the truth and to 'walk one's talk' is another. On a pragmatic level the integration of thought takes place when we are aware of the different types of thoughts, sensory inputs, memories, feelings and emotions in such a way that we create a healthier, more organized system within the mind. In this way the mind can operate at its optimum without being stressed and burdened by unfinished thoughts or unprocessed ideas. The integration of incoming and outgoing mental materials takes place through the simple power of awareness. Once we become aware of them, we give them proper attention—and if needed—adequate space within the mind. Or we simply let them go.

This requires the development of a high level of awareness and for this it is imperative that we have a regular meditation practice.

Be mindful of all the little ways in which your mental energies dissipate, and the ways in which tiny bits of information enter your consciousness and form your perceptions, concepts and beliefs. We must catch the stray thoughts that come into our mind that have little relevance to what we are doing or thinking. There are myriads of strands of unfinished thoughts and sensory inputs that need to be sorted and completed. Integration involves processing or digesting experiences and thoughts, keeping that which nourishes us and discarding what does not. We have to control what passes through the doors of the mind. If we fail to do so we will experience a bloated sensation of poorly digested mental food and we will become confused, lose focus or simply feel uneasy within ourselves.

If we wish to integrate or connect different aspects of our daily life we must use absolutely everything—every mental state, every condition of life, every challenging person we meet— for our own growth, and see all challenges as opportunities to grow. Take the simplest of activities and spiritualize them, adding to them an element of awareness, a gentle touch, love and presence! Success in life and spiritual practice lies in the word integration. We must learn not to waste precious mental energy. Place the guard of wisdom and love at the door of your mind.

Make your life into a continuous spiritual exercise. Spiritual life is not lived only at set times. Contemplate frequently that your life is filled with infinite possibilities. Even though it is essential that we have a regular and steady practice of meditation and yoga, we need to expand our domain of practice. Ask yourself the following questions: "When does spiritual practice end and secular life begin?" "Why do I seem to lose the peace and centeredness I created at the beginning of the day? Is it because something has gone wrong in my day? Somebody was rude to me? I was late for work?"

There will always be interruptions and unexpected events in our day, difficult people to deal with, and yet none of this should be an obstacle in our practice. In fact each one of these situations should stimulate us to strive even harder. This step requires the integration of what we may call the sacred with the secular. Otherwise we will feel the stress of neither connecting nor reconciling the two seemingly diametrically opposed ways of life. Live a total life without compartments. Connect the isolated rooms of your life by building windows and doors.

Do not look for ideal places to practice or ideal people to live with. In the beginning of our training we need to have a meditation room and a regular practice but as we progress we take advantage of every situation and every place in order to master some aspect of our practice. The mind eventually needs to accept all situations as a training ground. This gives us tremendous self-confidence and makes us very resourceful.

In our effort to grow spiritually it is important not to fall into the trap of being preoccupied with or obsessed with our weaknesses or thought processes that we don't like. If we focus exclusively on our faults instead of rejoicing in our efforts we end up seeing ourselves through the wrong lens and being hard on ourselves. Remember that spiritual life, or any striving for that matter, does not follow a straight line. There will be ups and downs in our practice. But we must keep on striving and doing our best. Rome was not built in a day! In Sanskrit there is a saying, *bahu vighnaani shreyamsi*, meaning simply, *good deeds, or the path to God, are filled with many obstacles.* Our focus is to build the good within us and of course that includes the removal of negative thoughts and habits. If we focus exclusively on how to build and sustain the positive, and continue on the path of staying aware, the negative in us will be removed by itself. If we pay attention to the beautiful flowers, we are not aware of the compost and dead leaves. What you think, so you become!

There may be several weaknesses, but never mind! We know them too well! Neither dwelling on them nor being reminded of them helps. To dwell on negative thoughts is to empower them and to consent to their continued action; it is to affirm and give them perhaps in an unnoticeable and subtle way, their right to stay and proliferate. Do not to get tricked into believing that dwelling on negative thoughts will eliminate them. Instead think of them only for as long as is necessary to correct them. A positive attitude and strength of mind are developed simply by the practice of applying with renewed effort a positive way of seeing a situation. Think of strength and not weakness. Keep in your mind these kinds of positive thoughts as frequently as you can—the frequent will become constant!

EXERCISE I
THE BEGINNING OF THE DAY

Is there such a thing as a good way to start the day? Yes! How we start the day has a profound effect on the rest of the day. We often say, "I got up on the wrong side of the bed!" What do you do first thing in the morning? Here are some suggestions:

Wake up as early as possible, since this period of time is usually in our control and our mind is in a luminous state. Open your heart to the messages from life and connect with manifold benevolent energies, entities and beings.

Stop the mind in its tracks if it starts to give you wrong suggestions about the nature of your life or the problems that may lie ahead. Let go of the tendency to worry. Use your imagination only to nurture inspiration and faith. Search for inspiration within your heart by looking forward to a feww small achievements, small loves, small concentrations, small conquests over your mind.

As you open your eyes concentrate on the feeling of simply being, recognizing that Presence of your innermost Being, which is silently always with us but of which we are rarely aware. We tend to take our existence for granted. We don't give it much thought. Take advantage of these first moments of the day that are still relatively free of thought and enjoy the fact that you exist. Your existence is not an ordinary one. You will notice over time that your existence as Pure Awareness is full of power. The first step is to acknowledge that you are conscious.

The second step is to become aware of your breath, and feel the flow of the breath through your nostrils. Then let your eyes fall on an inspiring image such as a flower, a picture that inspires you or a photo of a sage or saint that brings up the association of divinity. Then arouse the feeling of gratitude for a new day, for another opportunity to experiment anew and to improve the way you live, think and act.

Then slowly step out of bed still holding onto the strong presence of your awareness where thoughts are still not active. In the bathroom too, take a moment to gently smile as you look at your image in the mirror. Stepping into the shower can be a wonderful way of connecting with the stream of life in the form of water. Water purifies, refreshes and lightens. Using your imagination, let the water cleanse all negative thought from your mind.

Once you are dressed you are ready to explore the source of true peace, strength and wisdom—your innermost Self. Make it a point to spend a few minutes in meditation or prayer daily. Then quickly go over the basic practices of the day such as keeping patient, remaining calm, forgiving. Remind yourself to keep relaxed, confident that whatever problems may arise in the day have their solution and that any event is meant only to add to your strength and power. This is essential, otherwise the world will take you by surprise with its intensity and ability to affect your mind. Bless the day and the possibilities the new day will bring into your life and bless also the difficulties.

EXERCISE 2
DURING THE DAY

Measure the level of vibration of your mind and ask yourself, "Does my mind feel light and joyful . . . or anxious, worried, heavy, or depressed?" If you are feeling down, simply decide to take a few steps to shift your mood by entertaining thoughts of joy and hope for a few minutes along with deep breathing. Do a few stretches, or repeat a few prayers and mantras, sing a chant, or read an inspiring poem or a piece of writing. You may want to read aloud, or say your prayers aloud in order to feel their vibration.

CHAPTER 8

TRAINING OF THE MIND

The mind must be trained first. Before that, you will find the same world anywhere you go.

Swami Sivananda

The philosophy that we are the authors of our life is indeed the most liberating. It gives us the impetus to strive onward for perfection and freedom. Thought is the originator of this vast universe. Right understanding of the mind is the key to having peace of mind, success in life and in our relationships. The mind, when cultivated properly, becomes our best friend and guide. The only solution to all problems—individual, collective, physical, emotional or mental—is *control over one's mind*. The greatest task indeed, the challenge beyond measure, the battle with no apparent victory, is in being able to control, transmute and transform the energies of the mind. Life passes us by, opportunities continuously slip away, mistakes are frequently made, and yet the mind has still not been understood or controlled! How mysterious, how wonderful is this mind! Control of the mind is really the greatest victory—the pinnacle of life.

The power of personality and the power of the mind are nothing but the expression of the most prominent and dominant thoughts that we have cultivated, whether positive or negative. This is a natural law. Natural laws cannot be circumvented. The bliss that ensues from the proper training of the mind surpasses the pleasures and prosperity of the three worlds. The highest bliss lies in knowing the mind and having mastery over it. If we can control even the smallest negative thought, have mastery over even a single desire, exert command over one of our mental processes, bring order to our feelings, emotions and thoughts, consciously build and express virtuous qualities, have the courage to renounce the unnecessary, and hear the inner voice of Truth, we will know the bliss beyond this world.

Discipline is the ability to translate our visions, dreams and intentions into palpable reality, making them our own experience. Discipline is not a hard-task master; it is the process of unifying the heart and mind in a common pursuit. Discipline requires that we forego the lesser for the higher, committing to a higher goal that will ultimately blossom into our strength and power. This is of utmost importance for success on the spiritual path. Discipline is not a straightforward, always upward path. Rather, it is a rocky and circuitous climb. Whenever we make up our mind to improve an aspect of ourselves, we find that sooner or later life presents obstacles; we appear to fail, and sense no progress. But we learn that mastery in any field takes place one step at a time and every failure on the path is simply a stepping stone to success. This is the story behind everyone's triumph. The first positive step to intense spiritual practice is right intention and resolution. The next step, which should follow immediately, is that of right effort or exertion.

True commitment to a spiritual life is the ability to translate our ideals into action. Commitment to an ideal is the single most responsible factor for success in spiritual life. Become someone of concentrated effort. Use every moment to perfect yourself. Don't waste your life trying to change others; they must follow their own path. Believe that every moment is an opportunity to practice, improve, change or simply comprehend and realize.

Develop strong determination. It is the most important factor which will contribute to the realization of your thoughts. There is nobody who will be able to withstand the power of your determined mind. You can realize everything.

Swami Sivananda

Determination is the product of the cultivation of awareness and discrimination. We need to be selective about the quality of thoughts we want to manifest and materialize. Once pure thoughts have the support of powerful determination they will bring about their own fruition very quickly. In spiritual life determination is equal to realization.

Treat yourself with reverence. Salute yourself. Give great respect and veneration to your true being. You are a child of the eternal divine Spirit, the immortal Universal Soul. You are a part of It. Do not take yourself lightly. I am in essence pure consciousness, the universal pure consciousness. Know this and be this and live ever to be in this state of consciousness.

Swami Chidananda

Self-acceptance can be one of the most difficult goals to achieve in our lives. How many of us dislike or reject our past and our present, our mistakes and disappointments, our experiences, our looks, talents or attitudes? We may be angry at and appalled by our own limitations and character flaws. We may simply be embarrassed about who and what we are. Our feet are stuck! It is important to understand that the unpleasant part of ourselves has its own reality. We all carry negativity in some form or other—anger, aggression, complexes about sexuality and self-worth and more. To pretend that they don't exist only creates more complexes, guilt and a split within the mind. As long the mind denies them there will be turmoil, inner struggle and torment in life.

It is important therefore that we do not suppress them. We must learn to deal with them constructively and compassionately and transform them into the tools and opportunities for growth. When we observe a child wrestling with emotions such as anger or sadness, we feel concern and tenderness. In this moment we are holding the child in our heart even if there is a tantrum from the child. We also need and deserve compassion and softness from ourselves.

When we learn to evaluate our own experiences we need to be objective, to create some distance from the very emotions and thoughts with which we identify. Train yourself to create a more positive perspective with every challenge that presents itself. Experience is the best teacher. There is no more powerful a teacher than one's own experience and painful experiences are at times the best teachers. However painful an experience may be, try to own it, trusting that it was sent to you for your own growth. Do not waste your precious energy resisting life or denigrating the past. Life is not about liking or disliking. It is about learning, paying debts, increasing knowledge, broadening wisdom, growing in love, developing intuition and scaling the heights of divinity. Acceptance does not mean passivity, but proactivity. Whatever the present moment offers, accept it as if you had chosen it. We know where we would like to be, but when we will get there exactly is not easy to answer. In fact, we never know how close we are to our ideal or goal. Our commitment is to keep striving and to let the results take care of themselves. Signs of progress are often subtle; it may be that the next failure is in fact the final step before success.

EXERCISE
ONE MINUTE IN THE DAY

- I will be free from all thoughts and let myself just be. There is joy in simply being.

- I will smile and cultivate joy even in the midst of challenges, changes and suffering. I will look at them as my messengers of light and wisdom.

- I will remember that I am Atman, Pure Awareness, objectless and thoughtless. I will remember that I am not my thoughts and feelings but their witness and thus bring peace and trust to my heart.

- I will think of all as my brothers and sisters, as manifestations of my own Self, or Divinity or one God.

- Just as there are countless cells in the body related to each other, just as there are countless stars in the sky communicating with each other, so also there are countless beings that are related to each other as an organic whole.

- I will live with integrity today. I will free my mind from all contradictions and make all my thoughts and feelings stream in a single direction—that of love and wisdom. My goal and my way will be on the same wavelength. When I want peace, peace will be the way. When I want to experience love, love will be the way.

- I will be complete and strong, a whole person, extending the quality of integrity to all details in life. Peacefully sweeping, washing, walking.

- I will not go back, undo, uproot or abandon conquered ground.

- I will live in truth.

- I will live in love and sympathy.

CHAPTER 9

PRINCIPLES OF RIGHT THINKING

It is essential to understand the role that the intellect plays in our mind. Even though we think all day long, many of us are unaware that there is a right method to develop the power of the mind, or more specifically, our thinking capacity. We must ask ourselves these questions, "What is the right way to think of something?" "How can I use the power of my intellect and the sensitivity of my heart to find out the truth about something?" "What is the best way to examine something, to discriminate and come to the best possible conclusions?" "What is the role of my intelligence?" Whether we are involved in a creative process, envisioning an idea, or trying to resolve a problem, we need to remember that thinking is a highly complex skill and can only be mastered over time by applying precise principles and techniques. A good thinker must have good skills of observation, concentration, discriminative ability, thought processing, logic, ability to relate cause and effect, control over imagination and, for spiritual purposes, a well-integrated and pure mind.

One of the most important aspects of correct thinking is to link a thought or action with its effect. We may not always be able to predict an effect but we must go as deeply as we can into the recesses of the mind and into the heart of our understanding to obtain the greatest benefit from our thoughts and actions. Right thinking includes not only the intellect but also embraces the heart. The intellect has a discerning capacity and the heart has an intuitive capacity. Wisdom and love must come into loving union in order for our life to be lived to its fullest.

The intellect engages in the process of analysis to acquire knowledge. We must train it so we can discriminate between positive and negative actions and their consequences, between that which elevates us and that which disheartens us. The role of the intellect is to distinguish between the signs and functions of the gunas (subtle forces) in our mind. As we have seen, tamas is associated with inertia, ignorance, indifference and weakness; rajas with greed, strong ego, struggle, attachment, pride and selfishness; and sattva with harmony, love, kindness, light and joy. We may be intelligent and able, but lacking a higher sense of ethics, we allow the intellect to lead us astray. The role of intelligence is to make correct judgments based on proper observation and with full awareness. And yet we must understand that intellect as a faculty has its limits. Since the work of the intellect depends on sensory input, it cannot by itself know the truth. Knowledge or truth is a synthesis that can only be known by the heart. We may call this intuition. Right thinking has its foundation in kindness, loving thoughts, truthfulness, purity and selflessness.

Have clear mental images. Only those who have the gift of clairvoyance can see the formation of mental images. Most of our thoughts are not well grounded. They move with tremendous speed due to the fluctuation of the mind; they come quickly, trample over one another, and slip away fast; they have little weight or depth. The images in our mind are vague, unclear and poorly defined and for most of us, distorted. There is often a great deal of confusion in the mind. It is only able and mature thinkers, philosophers and *yogins* who have welldefined, clear, mental images. Strengthen your mental images by deep, logical, methodical thinking, reflection and meditation. Make your thoughts settle down and crystallize into definite forms.

Then whatever ideas you may hold related to your business, relationship, or philosophy will become firm.

There are generally four or five thoughts that appear to occupy our attention around the same time. We need to recognize them, organize them according to the order of their importance and act immediately on the ones that need to be addressed. Learn to intercept the tendency of grouping different thoughts together randomly; recognize when you are unaware of exactly what you are thinking. To think clearly we have to slow down the thinking process and control the emotions. The ability to concentrate well, strong will power and keen memory develop from clear thinking. Know at every moment what thoughts are present in your mind. Abandon the negative and select a positive thought, and let its form be vivid and well-defined.

Think steadily. Steady thinking implies the absence of erratic or random thinking. It is the ability to concentrate on a desired subject and its different aspects for a period of time. It is the control of the mind's tendency to wander off on another subject. Each time your mind wanders, gently and firmly bring it back to the subject in question. Do this for five minutes at a time. Other thoughts will arise, perhaps even important messages. Simply write them down quickly and come back to the subject. Take up another thought when you have exhausted the previous one. With this practice you will develop steady and organized thinking; you will be able to form strong, clear, welldefined mental images.

Think non-emotionally. Emotions are important but we cannot let them color our thinking processes; we must be even more vigilant when our mind is affected by negative emotions. When this is the case take time away from the train of thought and come back to it when your mind has calmed down.

Think constructively. It is important to examine the thinking process itself, to see whether or not it follows a correct line of argument. We should analyze a subject from different viewpoints so that our understanding of it is enriched and complete. Constructive thinking is when we build information as if building a house—one brick or one piece of information or argument at a time—sustaining a positive attitude as we do so. We then bring all the information together and come to a conclusion. And then we act upon it. The most important step is to follow up on a conclusion. Our mind is filled with myriad strands of unfinished thoughts. It is important to bring our thoughts to a conclusion so that they can be placed away tidily in our mental factory. Finalize each thinking process. Your mind will feel like an ordered and clean room in which every object has its own place.

Each one of us has our own particular 'background of thought'. We all have thoughts that occupy our attention throughout the day that may not have any relationship to the activity we are performing. Background of thought is the primary focus of the mind when not fully concentrated on a task at hand; it is a thought or an image to which we return frequently. A positive background is something that we love and look forward to being in its presence. It serves to uplift as well as anchor and stabilize the mind when facing different situations in life. A negative background however, makes us obsessive. For example, a mother may be at work and yet her mind will ever be going back to thoughts of her own children. A businessman thinks of his deals even when spending time with friends. A doctor thinks of her patients, even when relaxing at home. Someone looking forward to a vacation will have the trip as the background of thought. Strive to have a pure and uplifting background of thought. Choose to come back frequently to a lofty ideal, a mantra, your breath or anything that inspires you.

Stop daydreaming! To achieve success and happiness in life we must learn to live in and focus on the present. To daydream is a common habit, but when we look closely, we see it comes not from a lucid state of consciousness nor from being present. Daydreaming can bring us to mental states and situations over which we cannot easily exercise conscious control. We can find ourselves unprepared for the intrusion of negative emotion or thought. To counteract it we need to develop awareness and control over our imagination. When you think have a mental 'timer' on the go. Give yourself the amount of time you need to attend to particular thoughts, but no longer.

The mind by its very nature fluctuates and the moment it manifests, depending on its extent and nature, the power of imagination arises simultaneously. The illusion of the world around us is caused by this fluctuation of the mind. Its cessation is the goal of spiritual practice. Fluctuation sets the mind in motion and imagination expands on it. Imagination feeds worry, fear, anger and numerous mental ills and like an ocean full of powerful tides, exerts a great force on the mind, dragging it into its immeasurable depths. Imagination has many negative effects on the mind including exaggeration, magnification of perceptions and making mountains out of molehills. Victory over negative imagination means victory over destructive emotions. Since negative imagination animates and distorts the mind we must cultivate our imagination in such a way that it is used only for the positive. The wings of imagination are immense. When we carefully observe our mind we see that there is hardly a perception, or 'bare attention' that is not accompanied by and overpowered by the imagination. We see the object, not in its pure state, but 'contaminated' by our imagination. When we perceive an object it is the suggestive power of the imagination that turns it into something beautiful or ugly.

If not governed by constructive thought, the imagination will always magnify and exaggerate our troubles and weaknesses.

Yet when used in the right way imagination is a saving grace, a great tool; when used incorrectly it leads us to fear, despair, anger, jealousy and manifold illusions. For example if we succumb to the force of negative imagination, we can perceive a hugely reprehensible quality in one who in reality has only a slight weakness. Imagination is like wearing colored glasses or glasses with dense lenses—we are unable to see things clearly. The control of negative imagination is one of the most important practices in managing our thoughts and emotions.

Soar high on the wings of positive imagination and let your best thought do the work for you. If you think, "I can't," you won't! In order to achieve success, the first step is to enlist the cooperation of our true Self. The 'can'ts' and the doubts are the utterances of the lower, mechanical, habitual mind. Ignore them. As you practice the Pebble-in-the-Shoe exercise, you will extract yourself from their overwhelming influence. Stop and think carefully, observing your thoughts several times daily. Notice the power of exaggeration from today. You will be amazed to see how the mind adds to every truth. What is worry but the work of imagination? What is experienced as fear is our imagination given free rein. Banish ALL fear, ALL doubt. Do not harbour doubt in the name of logic and so-called reality. Believe that you are meant to succeed and the whole universe will support you.

Choose love. The mind must consult the heart. True love makes no mistakes. A student of mine once asked me for advice on making a difficult decision. I replied, "Ask as if love was the only judge. What would love do in this situation?" We must apply this principle in our daily lives. To work with the mind can at times be daunting. The enthusiasm required to gain mastery over the mind does not come easily; we need to approach our mind as if it were a child, and show it compassion, love and self-acceptance.

Say only that which you wish to materialize. Let your words be the means of realization. Be discriminative in what you say and how you say it. Words are audible thoughts; they are the manifesting power of our thoughts.

Remember—today is the day! Plan something each day that will bring you closer to your ideal. And here the size of your step is not as important as the nature and the direction of your effort. When the habit of aspiration is formed, all undesirable qualities and negative habits will fade away; they will die from lack of nourishment. Strive to rise a little higher each day. If you are completely satisfied with the life you are living, with the work you are doing, with the thoughts you are thinking, with the dreams you are dreaming, with the character you are building, you may be sure that the qualities of your mind and your spiritual life have started to deteriorate. Be aware that we can become complacent with our own practice; sometimes initial success acts like an opiate and puts us to sleep. A little more and a little higher than the day before is the secret of progress!

CHAPTER 10

THE POWER OF THE SUBCONSCIOUS MIND

If you want to cure yourself of a defect or a difficulty, there is but one method: to be perfectly vigilant, to have a very alert and vigilant consciousness.

The Mother

To gain complete mastery over our thought processes we must understand three important aspects of our mental activities: the subconscious mind, the will and the imagination. We have infinite riches within our reach. If we know how to access this wealth we can live a meaningful, joyous and abundant life. Our subconscious mind holds the solution to many of our problems. It is molded moment by moment by incoming impressions and by the quality of our thought. When life and thoughts are harmonized we find great support in the subconscious mind. The inner creates the outer; the world within creates the world without.

The subconscious mind is the seat of incredible powers. It governs the autonomic physical and mental processes that are responsible for birth, growth, decay and death. The instinctive mind, common to plant, animal and human, is found within the subconscious mind. Instincts are part of nature, necessary for our survival and as such we should not interfere with their work. However the lower emotions such as the instinctive drives of anger, greed and lust need to be controlled and sublimated.

Examples of how we have encroached on and impeded the protective work of our instincts include eating when we are not hungry; drinking water when we are not thirsty; not resting when we are tired; dressing inadequately when it is cold. Nature is quiet in the early morning hours, but we have become restless and are active at that time. In the evening when we start to yawn, this is a signal from Mother Nature to sleep, but most of us stay awake. The natural instinct of a child is to refuse meat and yet we insist on its consumption. We were not born with an instinct to smoke or drink alcohol. We know this from our first reaction to smoking—violent coughing—as the body tries to rid itself of the poison. The first time we take alcohol there is a feeling of nausea. The list is endless. We have managed to destroy many of our instincts by unnatural living and unwise choices and as a result have brought upon ourselves a host of illnesses, detrimental habits and mental problems. We must learn to retrain and trust our instincts. With the help of the subconscious mind we can change our negative patterns of behavior.

Some principles of the workings of the subconscious mind:

- Our subconscious mind is never at rest. Even while we sleep it arranges, analyses, compares, sorts out all facts and figures, works out the best solutions and finally carries out our requests and commands. It has the power to remind us to make a call or to wake us up at a particular time. When we set an intention to get up at a certain time in the morning, it is our subconscious mind that has the ability to wake us.

- Our subconscious mind is very sensitive to our conscious thoughts. It interprets our words literally. It operates without reasoning.

- All our conscious thoughts descend into the subconscious where they crystallize into character traits, habits and beliefs. Once we have learned an action through the intellect the subconscious mind takes over and performs the action automatically. Many of our daily activities—walking and driving are examples—are performed through the subconscious mind. It is referred to as the habit mind.

- The influence of the subconscious mind is subtle. We are under the impression that we think and act consciously but there is a tremendous input from our subconscious. In fact it is inestimable how much influence from the subconscious is expressed in our conscious actions.

- Once the subconscious mind has accepted an idea or a suggestion, it begins to execute it immediately.

- All that we have seen, heard, enjoyed, tasted, read and known from innumerable past lives, as well as our experiences from this life are lodged in the subconscious mind in the form of impressions.

A suggestion is similar to planting a seed; it is the act of putting an idea into the mind. It is a psychological process by which a thought or idea is taken in, accepted and put into effect. Within us lies a world that we barely know. Only occasionally are we aware that we have convictions, fears, beliefs and opinions that have developed from a long process of programming and conditioning. This deep inner molding rules our lives to a much greater extent than we can ever imagine. The suggestions and influences we have received during this life and previous lifetimes through our parents and ancestors are powerful forces that govern our lives. But remember that a suggestion has no power in and of itself; its power manifests when it is accepted mentally. For suggestion to work it has to be accepted by some part of our being. This is such a subtle process that it is rarely caught or analyzed by our intellect. Note well that our conscious mind has the power to reject a suggestion.

Media and advertising are obvious sources of suggestions but there are others such as the art we see, the poetry we read, the philosophy we study, the people we meet. The most important factor to bear in mind when considering what we are allowing ourselves to be influenced by is its quality. Artists in any field of endeavour must connect to the world of beauty and harmony and tune their minds to the most sublime energies in order to create a positive effect on the world at large. More and more we see discordant vibrations in the form of strange movies, chaotic music and capricious art which only adds to the negative energy of the world. If you are a creator, an artist of any kind, you have a responsibility! It is through the medium of the creative act that you translate the quality of your thoughts into visible form. Let us create only such things that will make this world and the universe an abode of peace, harmony and love.

Suggestions have a power of their own and we should give positive suggestions particularly to frightened, weak or ill people, children, pregnant women and the elderly. We should also be sensitive to the kind of suggestion we are giving when we are inquiring about someone's life, or when writing an e-mail or blog. Refrain from giving comments that would make a person worry or be frightened such as, "You don't look so well this morning." Our subconscious mind is susceptible and impressionable at these times:

- Upon waking and before falling asleep

- At meal times

- When in contact with water or near fire

- At times of prayer and meditation

- During sexual acts

- When ill or dying

It is customary for prayers to be said for example before and after a meal or during the time of transition.

Advertisers study how the subconscious mind can be manipulated in order to better sell their goods and services. Advertisements focus on arousing or creating illusory feelings, good or bad. As we move into the era of artificial intelligence, there is now a vast industry concerned with targeting our minds— through the internet—with an incessant stream of advertising, subliminal or otherwise. Programmers use algorithms to track our shopping habits and interests, using this information to suggest 'appropriate' products for purchase. We live in a world where we are preyed upon and targeted. Advertisements appeal to our basic instincts of self-preservation, self-image, our desires for sex and food, and promote sensuality and false promises of happiness and pleasure. Advertising is one of the most powerful external stimuli that incites our imagination. And the daily torrent of news in the media amplifies the negative impressions and fear that already exist in our minds. Be selective and reduce your exposure to news and television.

It is extraordinary how many people enjoy watching violent and sexual movies. These powerful images form deep impressions in us of insecurity, fear, anger, violence, unrest, darkness, despair and hopelessness which eventually translate themselves into our future choices of thoughts, feelings and actions. There are many instances where someone who committed a violent act, later confirmed that a movie or a video game had 'inspired' them. There are studies showing that what we watch affects not only our minds but also the cells of our body. In one particular experiment subjects watched on screen a person being stabbed in the stomach and it was found that those watching suffered minuscule perforations to their stomach membrane. We need to be very careful what we expose ourselves to.

Thoughts of hatred and lust produce the distorted images in the mind, and cause clouded understanding, perversion of intellect, loss of memory and confusion.

Swami Sivananda

All words, since they are a manifestation of thought, have power. It is essential to be aware of words that give us more confidence and strength and of those that have a debilitating effect on us. Try to use expressions such as, "I can do it," "My will is strong,"and, "I can do absolute wonders," and make the words penetrate your inner being. Challenges will become easier. Negative words are often repeated unconsciously in our minds, and so escape the scrutiny of our gate-keeping intellect. Without our knowledge such words play havoc within and without. Note the following negative expressions and their positive substitutes:

- *Impossible* replace with *Everything is possible.*

- *I can't* with *I will make an effort.*

- *This is difficult* with *It will become easier if I give it a try.*

- *This is stronger than me* with *This is a good challenge for me.*

- *I can't help it* with *It's the effort that counts.*

- *I will never be able to do this* with *I have done many 'impossible' things before.*

- *I can't help myself* with *I am in control of my life moment by moment, if I remember that I have a choice.*

- *I am stuck* or *I am blocked* with *I will take the first step.*

- *I am sick of it* with *I have to develop patience and understanding towards this.*

- *I would rather die than do this* with *I would prefer not to do this.*

- *You drive me crazy* with *You have upset my mind.*

- *Things are getting worse* with *It is just a process and I am working on it.*

- *I see no way out; it is hopeless* with *I don't know the answer yet. I will remain hopeful.*

Avoid using vulgar language and swear words, they are pervaded with aggressive and toxic energy. Purify your expressions by making them less emotionally-charged, and more accurate, kind and purposeful. Avoid ambiguous expressions such as "As far as," and, "I will do my best". They block the creative energy of your conscious mind and stun the subconscious mind. Be aware of the following negative suggestions when communicating with others: "You can't." "You'll never amount to anything." "You'll fail." "You haven't got a chance." "You're all wrong." "What's the use." "Nobody cares." "There's no point in trying so hard." "It's too late now."

If you hear frequent complaints from others such as "The economy is really bad," and "Life is so tough," and similar, protect your subconscious mind by not reacting, neither agreeing nor disagreeing, just staying quiet; if not, your subconscious mind will be influenced, absorbing the negativity.

Autosuggestion is when we give ourselves a suggestion or affirmation. The main principle behind this practice is that the suggestions are to be given frequently, in a relaxed manner and embraced with faith. When feeling accompanies autosuggestion it becomes a powerful force, helping us to retrain, remold and re-educate the subconscious mind, and enabling us to open ourselves up to a more harmonious and positive life. We communicate indirectly with our subconscious mind by using autosuggestion. As we repeat a statement or affirmation, and pour our heart's feeling into it, our subconscious mind absorbs it and soon acts up-on it. Since the subconscious mind does not reason it does not question or doubt the nature of the suggestion. We can repeat autosuggestions aloud, whisper them or repeat them mentally. We can also write them down on paper or listen to them.

An autosuggestion may not be effective if at the very moment we recite it we are experiencing a strong, opposing emotion which is fully active and predominant in our mind. It is very difficult to arouse a positive feeling when our mind is already filled with very strong negative thoughts. The autosuggestion will have no impact if we are tense or under pressure. For example saying, "I am calm and patient," when the mind is very angry will make controlling the mind difficult. If our mind is filled with depressing thoughts it is hard to replace them with opposite thoughts of joy. The practice of replacing the negative with the positive is only efficient when the negative thoughts are weak.

For autosuggestion to work we need to be in a positive, relaxed state of mind. The mind needs to be in a soft, nurturing space. Then the subconscious mind becomes a fertile soil for the seed of positive change to grow. The first step is to lessen the effect of the existing negative impressions in the mind by using the will. At times like this, this process will feel like a tug-of-war but eventually victory will be ours. This is how the power of autosuggestion operates. If we persist long enough in maintaining correct thought and the corresponding mental attitude we will experience the magic of yoga. Generally we do not believe sufficiently in the power of our thoughts or the mental images and the feelings we hold. To change the angle of vision means to change our thoughts and our state of mind or attitude (*bhava*).

Assume a comfortable posture and relax your body completely. Let go of all thoughts but the ones concerning your affirmations. Repeat your affirmations with a deep, relaxed, gentle, loving and convincing voice over and over again for about ten minutes every morning and evening. As you put your heart into the affirmations and you start to build an emotional connection with them, stronger and stronger impressions will be made in your subconscious mind and you will slowly find that the affirmations are molding into the reality of what you want to become.

A great portion of our subconscious mind is made up of layers of submerged experiences which can be brought to the surface of our conscious mind by means of concentration. Swami Sivananda speaks of "the technique of speaking to one's subconscious mind and the art or science of extracting work from it". We must treat the subconscious mind with respect to make it collaborate. It is only then that it will lend its help and give us the knowledge we need. It is a question of practice and practice makes perfect. If we remain persistent and methodical we will harness its considerable powers and solve problems much more efficiently. When a problem presents itself we tend to become tense and agitated. The secret to solving a problem is to remain as relaxed as possible, allowing the subconscious to assist us in finding the solution. Even though the mind is relaxed, we must still keep it keen and attentive as we resolve the problem. You will be surprised to see how magnificently the subconscious works and in such a mysterious manner!

When you are unable to solve a problem in life or you want to find the answer to a scientific or philosophical question, ask your subconscious mind to help you, giving it your full trust and confidence and you are bound to get the right solution.

Give it a command or make a request in the following manner: "My friend, subconscious mind! I want the solution, to this riddle or problem very urgently tomorrow morning. Kindly do it quickly." Let your command be given in very clear terms, free of ambiguous words such as maybe or I hope. The answer may come the next morning. But sometimes it may be busy, in which case you will have to wait for some time. Just keep repeating the same request every day at the same time. There is a great transformative power in intention, a charged thought. The secret of success is to practice the method again and again—you are bound to succeed.

Your conduct during the day influences and molds the subconscious mind. Begin the process of re-educating your mind by conscious cultivation of your best thoughts while in the wakeful state. Have a regular spiritual practice such as the practice of meditation, self-introspection and yoga. Find a spiritual center or organization with which you feel a connection. Spiritual practice and spiritual company are a great way to charge the subconscious with new and positive ideas.

Many of us are slapdash and inattentive in the way we do things, careless about our language or the quality of our thought. Develop precision in your actions and words. Think deeply and then act accordingly. Finish incomplete projects. Get things done and organized.

Harmony is what our subconscious mind likes the most! Positivity, enthusiasm, purity and rhythm are just some of the qualities that nurture and keep our subconscious mind in the state of optimum health and integration. To create more harmony in your personality, establish higher standards in your ethics. Create rhythm and regularity in all your actions, feelings and thoughts. Everything in life follows a plan and rhythm. If your life is erratic it will negatively influence the subconscious mind.

Let your whole personality emanate an aura of integrity, truth and purity. Be true to yourself first. Do what you say. If you live in truth there will be no conflict, no division in your thinking and you won't need additional energy to maintain the inaccuracy and falsity that you have created. When we lie our subconscious mind gets 'infected' and becomes subject to deep anxiety and worry and ceases to come to our aid.

Purify your subconscious mind by infusing it only with the choicest of impressions. Reduce the reading of the news and the internet, step away from gossip and negative thoughts about others, and surround yourself with the purest outpouring of thought in the form of inspirational and spiritual books, uplifting music and elevating art. Keeping reminders of wisdom around the house in the form of written positive affirmations will also help. Let the pictures, photos and any other visual symbols or objects in your home be of an uplifting nature. All these positive vibrations are necessary for a healthy subconscious mind.

Purify and sublimate your desires. It is the subconscious mind that holds the key to many of our frustrations, illnesses and deeply-held negative emotions and conditioning. Each suppressed desire acts like a dampener on our willpower and happiness. Desires can cause complexity and difficulty in our lives and we need to work out ways to sublimate those that are detrimental to our physical and spiritual wellbeing. Every unfulfilled desire keeps hold of a precious portion of our willpower within itself. The consequence is that we feel restless, agitated and generally unhappy. Leading a purposeful and selfless life based on spiritual principles will gradually help you sublimate all desires and remember that the more the sublimation, the greater the willpower.

Talk well about yourself. The subconscious will respond. Even though it is good and necessary to share our life issues with others, avoid burdening them with your problems. If you are experiencing health difficulties it is better not to concentrate or dwell too much on them or talk too much about them.

Many of us absorb unnecessary information from media and other people. Don't store useless information that can linger in the mind for hours or even days. Choose what to remember and what to discard. Spend a few minutes alone in silence every day. If this is not possible, then utilize whatever little time you have alone. Select a quiet place such as a riverbank, the top of a mountain, the open terrace of your house, a seashore, a simple meadow, a corner in a temple, church, mosque or room. As the mind is naturally attracted by the beauty of a place or landscape or by the deep silence of the location, it will be easy to let go of unnecessary thoughts. If you practice in your room you may want to burn incense, which will help you stay calm and alert.

The subconscious mind can be of great help in improving the qualities in your personality. Before going to sleep, concentrate on an image you would like to embody and say gently and clearly, 'I want to become the embodiment of kindness' (or any other quality), and the subconscious will help you turn that into reality.

Declutter. The subconscious mind serves the conscious mind and tries to make information available to it. With unfinished and unprocessed thoughts the mind becomes like a swamp. We accumulate and hoard many things: physical items, thoughts, emotions, experiences and memories. Everything we possess requires a certain amount of space in our mind. The mind is like a computer, storing information and programs. A life filled with clutter negatively affects the subconscious mind.

When we let go of things, whether physical or mental, the once-occupied space in the mind becomes available for new ideas and information and results in a release of energy. We feel lighter and happier. Go through your closet, desk, garage, medicine cabinet, bookcase—any cluttered storage area—and discard what you no longer need. Remember to simplify, simplify, simplify. Commit to owning less and you will find, all of a sudden, space opens up not only externally but internally too. To clear our physical space is a form of healing. You can also do a mental inventory, examining attitudes (prejudices, hatreds, resentments) stored within your psyche. When possible contact those with whom you harbor unresolved issues involving hurt, resentment, guilt or jealousy. Attempt to resolve them and then let them go. If you are unable to do so in this way, then write them down on paper, being as specific as possible. Then burn the paper symbolically releasing the content.

The essential element to consider when we are using the power of the subconscious mind is to have trust. We must learn to eliminate the distrust we have of ourselves. If we do not trust ourselves, by which we mean the subconscious mind, we cannot progress on our path. We must give the subconscious only precise, non-ambiguous, concrete, positive suggestions and affirmations, coupled with their application in daily life. We must keep the subconscious unpolluted through ethical practices such as love, compassion and truthfulness. We must always remember our potential as well as the potential of others. Time matters little here.

Remember to smile! You are now free!

EXERCISE 1
CONTEMPLATE THE LIFE OF AN IDEAL PERSONALITY

Contemplate the life of a perfect personality such as Jesus or Buddha and think of their deeds, their life and ideals. As a result your life will be filled by the qualities you contemplate, such as purity, courage and compassion. The thought will transform you into its own likeness. We become like that which we worship and what we think.

EXERCISE 2
THE PRACTICE OF JOY AND CHEERFULNESS

Repeat the following affirmations with sincerity and intense feeling:

• Joy is my natural state OM OM OM

• I smile and laugh OM OM OM

• I am cheerful OM OM OM

• I am full of good spirits OM OM OM

• I am lively and full of gladness OM OM OM

• I am pure joy OM OM OM

Repeat mentally *OM Joy* several times. Smile and laugh several times. Practice cheerfulness during the day. Manifest it in your daily life. Feel that you actually possess cheerfulness, radiating joy all around. Repeat *OM Joy, OM Cheerful*, mentally, daily several times. Gradually within a few weeks or months dejection and depression will be replaced by joy and cheerfulness.

EXERCISE 3
ELIMINATING FEAR

It is very difficult to combat fear directly as it is powerful and deeply embedded in our psyche. Many of us have been victims of this negative trait over many lifetimes. Now is the time to put the seed of courage in your heart and allow it to grow. Fear will die by itself. Our true nature is Pure Awareness, which is beyond the body and mind. We are seldom aware of our innermost Being, the simple presence that is felt behind our thoughts and feelings. All our fears are due to our perception of 'other' or 'otherness', commonly known in philosophy as duality. In reality we are one with all. Separation and divisions, including the perception of objects, are all due to our ignorance of who we truly are. We identify primarily with our body and the mind. But our innermost Self knows no fear and meditation on that immortal aspect of us removes all fears. Starting today, don't think of yourself as the body. Instead, identify yourself with your all-pervading, immortal, fearless Self (*Atman*). Be patient as the conquest over the stubborn habit of body-mind identification cannot be achieved in a day or a week. Constantly think of yourself as *Atman* and you will gradually become fearless. The more you think of your true Self, the more courageous you will become. Meditate. Assert. Recognize. Realize:

• I am fearless, all-pervading Atman or Being OM OM OM

• I have no fear of anything OM OM OM

• Courage is my birthright OM OM OM

• I behold the one Atman (Self) everywhere OM OM OM

• Everything is my own Self OM OM OM

Find additional affirmations from the scriptures or inspirational writings.

EXERCISE 4
PRATIPAKSHA BHAVANA—MEDITATION ON PATIENCE
(ADAPTED FROM SWAMI SIVANANDA)

Introspect and take a look at your character for a couple of minutes. Select a negative quality you want to reduce and eliminate. Now identify the opposite quality. In order to eliminate fear meditate on courage, for anger choose patience or forgiveness. Let us say that you are frequently affected by anger; start to develop your understanding and contemplation of its opposite, patience. The practice should be done daily for some time. The practice consists of contemplating different aspects of the quality of patience each day taking a different idea. Early in the morning, sit in a comfortable position and begin to think of the virtue patience, its importance, its merits and its healing effects. Think of the best ways of how you can implement it into your daily life and imagine doing your common tasks with more patience. Consider how you are going to maintain its practice when in challenging situations, such as the ones when you feel provoked, tired or stressed. Take one of each of these aspects for your daily contemplation. Today think of the importance of patience, the next day about its practice. It is important to sustain the train of thoughts so that you think of it as steadily as you can, recalling the mind when it wanders.

Now create an image of yourself as being a perfect model of patience and end with the practice with a vow, "This patience is my true nature; from today I will cultivate and express patience in everything I do." Write on several pieces of paper, *Om Patience* and hang them in prominent places in your home. For a few days probably there will be no a visible change. You may still feel irritable. But go on practicing steadily every morning and applying it every day. Soon you will see the sign of improvement that manifests like a flash of memory. You may still get annoyed by things and not be able to let immediately go of the feeling of anger, the thought will suddenly flash in your mind unbidden: "I should have been patient." This is the first step! Continue with your practice. You will soon be able to stop the outer manifestation of the impulse of impatience. Continue with the practice. The irritable impulse will grow feebler and feebler until you find that irritability has disappeared and the patience has become your normal attitude towards annoyances. In the same manner you can develop virtues such as sympathy, self-restraint, purity, humility, benevolence, nobility, generosity and of course more.

EXERCISE 5
MEDITATION ON COURAGE AS A VIRTUE

Close your eyes and breathe deeply and slowly. Inhale for three seconds and exhale for three seconds. Continue to breathe deeply for some time until you feel calm and relaxed. Now visualize a moment in time when you felt fearful. Try and picture perfectly where you were at the time, and the people or the incident that involved this fear. Focus on their faces and the surroundings to bring the strength of the memory back to you. Remember specifically how your body felt. Remember the thoughts and feelings that came up as a consequence of this fear. Now think of the disadvantages which fear brought into this particular situation and also life in general. Think about the debilitating nature of fear as opposed to the restorative nature of courage. Now go back in your mind's eye to the scenario and enact the whole situation visualizing yourself acting with courage. See the difference that the feeling of courage would make in your thoughts, feelings and behavior. Acknowledge in your body and your mind how it feels to be courageous. Now picture the word COURAGE in large clear letters in your mind and focus on the meaning and the power of the word as you continue to breathe slowly and deeply. Visualize yourself as strong, calm and courageous. Consider and absorb the advantages that courage brings and what it will enable you to do or achieve in this situation and in your life. Repeat OM COURAGE three times or more times and feel the new strength coming into your being with each repetition. You feel peaceful, strong and courageous.

EXERCISE 6
GIVING UP NEGATIVE HABITS

You can change any habit by patient effort and perseverance by simply creating a new habit. Impressions of the old habit will remain but through the power of determination the impressions of the new habit will overcome their influence. For example you can change the style of your handwriting and by applying a new mode of thinking, you can change your destiny. People of great will power conquer negative habits by mere intention. The whole of nature comes under the control of one of such tremendous will. Try to increase your willpower by all means available.

The most effective method of overcoming a negative habit is by ridding yourself of it in one stroke—in not indulging in it any longer. "Nothing succeeds like success"—there is no easier way of giving up a bad habit than giving it up! For example if you want to stop smoking, the best way to do it is to throw away the cigarettes and say, "I will no longer smoke," and keep the mind busy on projects and spiritual practices. The demands of the lower nature will be strong and its voice loud, but keep on with the good work! This is the most effective method—but not necessarily suitable for the majority of people.

A more gradual method of dealing with negative habits is to write on paper your wish to give up the negative habit in the form of a prayer to the Divine. Under the prayer write down your insights and conclusions about how the habit has been affecting you negatively. Read the note early in the morning and just before going to bed. Think about it for a while. Rotate the ideas in your mind. Let them sink deeper and deeper into your subconscious. Let your conviction about giving up the habit grow stronger and stronger. Then state the intention in your mind, "I must give up this negative habit." Offer a prayer to the Divine to help you. Even though you have not actually given up the habit, when you indulge in it you will first experience a decreased pleasure from it, then you will feel indifference or non-attachment, and finally at the end, repulsion.

It is important as you go along that you inquire into the nature of the habit, emphasizing the negative effect it exerts on your life. Increase other spiritual practices. Certainly do not fight the habit; it will only weaken your will power. Stay away as much as possible from the temptation created by constant indulgence; temptation is simply unconquered desire. Remain a safe distance from that which tempts you—there is no other way in controlling the mind. You cannot fight the habit and at the same time have temptation nearby. It is like dealing with fire; each time you come too close it will burn you, you will be knocked sideways each time. Even if you fail in your attempts, take a moment to reflect why and then recommit.

CHAPTER 11

DEVELOPING WILLPOWER

*Every thought that is controlled, every desire that is trans-
formed, every weakness that is eradicated will add strength to
the mind, will develop your will and take you one step nearer to
the goal. Fight bravely! Come out victorious and wear the spiritual laurels of divine wisdom, eternal peace and supreme bliss.*

Swami Sivananda

The freedom is the freedom of the will before it was bound.

Swami Vivekananda

Willpower is the ability to pursue goals and execute tasks regardless of the nature of obstacles, discomfort or difficulties. By applying our will we are able overcome challenges, temptations, our
negative tendencies, and any resistance in our nature.

There is a world of difference between will and desire; in fact
they are opposite in their action and scope. A desire is a tiny
ripple in the ocean of the mind, whereas will is that power
which executes the very desires. Will is the power of choosing
or determining. Desire pertains to the mind; will is characteristic of our Self—the Universal Consciousness. Desire is personal; will is cosmic or universal.

When our innermost Self determines the activities, un-influenced by attractions or repulsions towards circum-stances and people, the will is manifested. When outer attractions or repulsions determine the activity and the person is drawn hither and thither by these, deaf to the voice of the Self, unconscious of the Inner Ruler, then the desire is seen.

Swami Sivananda

To develop willpower is the essence of life. We may have many talents but if we lack willpower we will not succeed. Conversely, if we have a lesser talent but are endowed with great willpower we see a path opening before us and are crowned with success. Will is a dynamic soul-force; it is what we are made of. It is ultimately who we really are. Will is that power that executes desires; it crystallizes our ideas, thoughts and visions into concrete forms and experiences; it is a tangible reality. Negative thinking weakens willpower. But if the will is made pure and strong then we can accomplish greatness. It is by exercising our will that we make choices and determine the best for others and ourselves.

What are the signs of strong and weak willpower? How does lack of willpower manifest in daily life? Most of us have no program for life, making it hard to focus. We give up easily and have difficulty making decisions or standing up for what we believe in. We suffer from fear and worry. Depression and negativity are both signs of weak or compromised willpower. Those with strong will are calm and cheerful. They have a gift, a capacity to tackle challenging situations with steadiness and minimum delay. They rarely leave things to be accomplished later or by somebody else and can influence others easily. Stronger minds influence weaker minds. Is your life moving in the direction you want it to? If so, you have strong willpower. It doesn't matter how many difficulties you have, your will clears the way.

Be ever resolute and unwavering in building a new life for yourself. Even the smallest of actions count. We are molded moment by moment, first on the level of our thoughts and then of our action. Resoluteness and the power of renewal are what are most needed. We must remind ourselves of the choices we have in order to break the old, dark patterns within our minds. If only we could will it strongly enough! Of all actions the actions of love count the most. So speak your heart, and speak it with no fear. Our life should be guided by a definite principle. Just as we have a plan for the day, a business or travel plan, so also we must have a plan for our whole life. We must investigate and find out what and who we are and what we would like to become and then work hard to attain the goal with courage and sincerity of purpose. And remember that whatever you want to become, you can become today, and if not for the whole day, at the very least for one minute a day!

Will is truly the king of mental powers. When the will is active, all the mental powers, such as power of judgment, power of memory, power of grasping, power of holding, reasoning power, discriminating power, power of inference, power of reflection—all these come into play within a split of a second. They come to aid the willpower, their master.

Swami Sivananda

Willpower is not developed by thinking but by action.

Swami Vishnudevananda

There are some well-defined principles behind the use of willpower.

Will is like a muscle—it can be developed only by use, without which it atrophies and leads to weakness and loss of purpose. Will is weakened by the influence of cravings and desires that are not in alignment with our higher needs. When will is made pure and strong through the sublimation of selfish desires, it works wonders. But for many of us the will is weak due to the influence of the dissipating power of so many desires. When a desire is controlled, it is transformed into will. Use your will only for positive actions. It is always advisable to reserve the will-force for the achievement of spiritual goals. Concentrate exclusively on what you want to achieve and don't think of your weaknesses. Do not test the strength of your will in the very beginning. Wait patiently until it becomes strong and pure. It will take time. Practice will make you perfect. Experiences will help you and teach you.

Development of our will is a necessity and an imperative. But how do we develop willpower?

You take one little thing, something you want to do or don't want to do. Begin with a small thing. If, for instance, there is a habit or a virtue you want to develop, you insist on it with the same regularity—you insist on it and compel yourself to do it—as you compel yourself to lift a weight. You make the same kind of effort, but it is more of an inner effort.

The Mother

Work with resolves. Make a few at the beginning of each month and at the start of the new year and systematize your practices around them. The most simple and easiest way to achieve this is to regulate your routine and keep to it religiously every day. Keep up a daily spiritual diary, a daily journal of your practices. The resolves will become much more effective if you do so and your evolution will be rapid. Most importantly, think of your resolves as soon as you wake up and remind yourself of them a few times during the day. Take such resolves as the following and add more of your own:

- I will meditate every day.

- I will study my mind and will find out my strengths and weaknesses.

- I will strengthen my will.

- I will keep healthy.

For example make a daily routine for physical exercise and yoga. We must strive to attain the greatest standard of health. Keep the body strong and healthy by regular exercise and yoga practice and choose the best possible food to power the body. Make the routine according to your capacity. Don't bite off more than you can chew or you may give in to temptation and eventually give up. Focus only on a few exercises and do them faithfully every day. The real strength is the strength of resolve, of renewal.

EXERCISE
STRENGTHENING OF THE WILL

The following are practices that have a direct bearing on the strengthening of the will:

- Do a difficult task first. Say goodbye to all procrastination. Procrastination is the thief of time. Whatever you plan to accomplish daily, carry it out. Too much thinking is a hindrance to the development of the the will. It brings confusion and blocks the creative power of the mind. You may need time to decide on an action, but once you have made a resolve, exert your will immediately in order to accomplish it. The delay in exertion of will is truly detrimental for spiritual aspirants. Give up the illusion of 'next time'. Do it today, do it this hour, do it this moment. Do it now!

- Do something that is difficult for you to do and don't do something that is easy or not good for you to do.

- Avoid doing too many things at once. Avoid dividing your energy into too many projects. Learn to conserve your energy.

- Don't let the idea that your life may be a failure ever find its home in your mind or heart. Believe that you are meant to succeed.

- Develop your attention and endurance by transforming your negative thoughts, feelings and reactions, by sublimating anger, by fasting, and by remaining calm, resourceful and faithful in difficult times.

- Patiently listen to the words of others even though what they say may not be interesting or engaging.

- Train yourself to do actions or tasks that may appear to be uninteresting such as cleaning, cooking or other chores.

There are additional practices that are directly or indirectly related to the development of will.

Just as energy is wasted in idle talk and gossiping, so also energy is wasted in entertaining useless thoughts. Try to not waste even a single thought. Conserve all mental energy. Utilize it for higher spiritual purposes and for meditation and helpful service to humanity. Drive away from your mind all unnecessary, useless thoughts. Entertain only thoughts that are helpful and useful.

Swami Sivananda

Conserve your energy. All forms of energy within our body and mind are ultimately the soul-force or our true nature. These energies have only one source and that is of our nature as Pure Will or Pure Consciousness. We have numerous energies within us such as physical (muscular, skeletal), emotional (anger, fear), mental (thoughts and ideas) and sexual. When we learn to control them they are transmuted or sublimated into will-force. Our use of energy is connected to our desires. The fewer our desires, the stronger our will. Control of all energies goes back to the transmutation of sexual energy (*brahmacharya*). Sublimated sexual energy is the substratum of will.

Do not waste mental energy. We live in a time of excess and waste, not only in the world but also in the way we drain ourselves mentally and emotionally. One of the greatest challenges we face today is knowing how to employ the power of our thought. So many of us do not know what to allow into the mental factory and what to keep out, and we are constantly mulling over things that have no bearing on our spiritual and mental work. Study your thoughts and be selective about which to nourish and which to abandon. The cost of wasted mental energy is enormous. Our modern lifestyle with a plethora of gadgets and neverending entertainment has contributed to an increased loss of mental energy and power. Every thought, every action and sentiment has to have the highest purpose in life as its background. From the point of view of our potential, this is the only life we have. We have to protect ourselves from dissipation of the mind and from entertaining negative and powerless thoughts.

Work on reducing useless and wasteful thoughts that are diverting your energy from the main goal. Use your power of choice every moment and you will soon find that you are sailing steadily in the right direction. Have a plan to get rid of these thoughts. Ask yourself, "Do I need to think about this now? Is this the best way to think about the situation?" We waste our precious energy by judging others, dwelling on their faults and insisting they change. The energy we use to judge and attempt to change others is the very same energy we need to use to perfect ourselves and to live according to our own ideals. Train your mind in constructive, positive thinking that is free from fear, worry, unwise suggestions, obsession or failure.

Do not waste time. Wasting time means wasting life and wasting opportunities. We are already 'forced' to waste time when we wait at airports, at the doctor, in traffic jams, etc. We must use our time more efficiently for specific spiritual exercises. In addition our time is wasted when unnecessarily we spend time in restaurants, cinemas, shows etc.; engaging in all kinds of talk—political talk, gossip, empty talk; doubting; criticizing; hoping and waiting vainly for people and situations to change; worrying; doing too many things and/or not doing them on time; and our reactions—the most time is wasted on this!

Do not brood over failures, weakness and mistakes. Brooding weakens our will. There is always a suitable and effective method to overcome a crisis or a trying situation. Let the weakness remain there for some time. Reflect. Develop vigilance. When the will and understanding strengthen and purify they merge into a powerful force which no weakness can withstand.

Reduction of even one thought will give mental strength and peace of mind. You may not be able to feel this in the beginning, as you do not possess a subtle intellect; but there is a spiritual thermometer inside to register the reduction of even a single thought. If you reduce one thought, the mental strength that you have gained by this reduction will help you to reduce the second thought easily.

Swami Sivananda

Practice silence. Our culture has not yet discovered the joy and power of silence. Every experience is verbalized to excess. The energy conserved by reducing our speech and the amount we read can be a powerful transformative tool and a healing agent for our aching minds and souls. Silence teaches, reveals and heals. It is an aid to introspective life and meditation. It reveals to us the subtle ways of the mind. It slowly uncovers the truth behind our complex emotions. When problems and challenges become tiresome or unbearable we naturally descend into silence for healing and rejuvenation. Powerful insights are born in silence. During silence we can introspect and practice self-analysis. Watch your thoughts. You will gain more understanding of how your mind works. You will derive immense benefit from the practice of silence. There are several stages in the practice of silence—the greatest silence is the silence of the mind when we rest in our Awareness. Physical silence will eventually lead to the experience of silence of the mind.

Willpower is connected to all other mental capacities and is not separate from memory, attention and concentration.

Keep your memory in good working order. As we get older, we easily forget the names of persons and places. The mind remembers through association but with age the subconscious mind starts to lose its power of grasping and storing ideas. This is further exacerbated by constant mental work—reading, overwork, and emotional problems such as worrying. There are a few very good books on memory; those written by memory champion Dominique O'Brien are excellent. Pick up a few exercises and experiment with them. Keep a daily diary of your memory practices. This is very important. You can monitor your progress and correct your failures. Keep doing the memory exercises for at least a year and you will see how as your memory improves your willpower grows stronger.

Increase your powers of concentration. Do regular concentration exercises in the morning for fifteen minutes daily. Let your concentration be on spiritual objects such as symbols, mantras, images or reading from spiritual books. The practice of concentration will help immensely in the development of your memory and willpower.

Discipline the senses. This is an important aspect of training the will. If the senses are restless there can be no concentration. The senses make the mind go outward. Since the senses cannot operate independently from the mind their control is really the control of the mind.

Develop positive qualities and remove the negative. Make a list of qualities you feel you are lacking. For some of us it may be courage, for others, compassion. Each of us is different in what would make us complete. Perhaps you can identify four or five qualities in your character that are weak. Develop them one at a time. Make a positive quality a theme for each month and learn as much as you can about it, meditate on that quality every day and attempt to practice it all day long—you will soon develop and manifest that quality in your character. Since there is a magnetic effect of qualities, if you develop one important virtue all other virtues will come of their own accord. The development of virtuous qualities will itself remove most of the negative qualities. But aim for the eradication of negative qualities at the same time. This way your progress will be fast.

Use autosuggestion. Get up early in the morning and sit in a comfortable position. Meditate on the following sentences and repeat them mentally with feeling:

- My will is pure, strong and irresistible OM OM OM

- I can do anything through my will now OM OM OM

- I have an invincible will OM OM OM

Keep the mind calm and balanced under all conditions. A calm mind is unimaginable wealth! One who is calm is happy and strong. Even if you fail to stay calm many times in a single day, make a new resolve and try again and again, and then once again! You will soon taste the great fruit of equanimity and mental strength. If in addition you can keep your heart open like a child and smile, you will be on the road to becoming a sage! Always be your own master and make the best of things. If at times the circumstances seem to be stronger than you, settle into the inner silence and remember, "What cannot be cured must be endured. Even this will pass away."

Use correct language; be precise with your words.

Words possess tremendous power. By words you can encourage and cheer others; you can give the greatest happiness to others. By words you can ruin and displease others. By words the teacher imparts his knowledge to his students. By words the orator keeps his audience spellbound. Word is Brahman or God in manifestation. Be careful in the selection of your words. Use sweet words and conquer the hearts of others. Never use harsh words.

Swami Sivananda

If we knew the true power of our words we would rarely speak and speak only to bless and to console. Control over speech is control over the mind. Those who are able to control the power of speech have both time and energy to accomplish much and attract to themselves all manner of blessings. Great restlessness accompanies the unwise use of words. Hurts, disbelief, doubts, breakups of friendship, distress—even wars—all owe their birth to the wrong choice of words. The ability to control our words is a sure means to peace. Use only measured and well-chosen words in your writing and speech. In order to be effective with our words, we need to bring consciousness into a more awakened state before we speak. If we are able simply to rest in silence, in our inherent wisdom, even for a brief moment before we make an utterance, we will see that our words become infused with power. To gain the true power of speech we must practice truthfulness and non-violence. Speak measured words only.

Rise above blame. Do not blame challenging environments. Since we do not live in a perfect world and are surrounded by people and situations which challenge us, it will serve us well if we train ourselves to create our own positive mental atmosphere that is with us wherever we are. There are challenges in every place. They do not happen only in our own individual world. If we accept the fact that we must work on ourselves in this manner we will soon become strong and dynamic. This is a great secret.

The signs of a growing will are many and powerful. You will feel inner strength. You will have an unruffled mind and will feel joy welling up in your heart. You will not be puzzled by the appearance of challenges. Things that appear difficult will become simple. Matters that used to upset your mind in the past will no longer have an effect on you. You will be able to accomplish an amazing amount of work and tackle challenging situations wisely and fearlessly. You will learn fast and feel that your evolution as a spiritual being is quickening. You will create opportunities instead of waiting for them to appear. You will be able turn every action into an act of will, into an act of learning and success using them as a springboard to the highest goal. You will become fearless and you will be able to accept whatever comes your way. You will use the obstacles you face to show you what you need improve. Your walk will become graceful; you will feel free! Your speech will be powerful; the truth will resonate in your speech and demeanor, changing the way others think and live and teaching them to direct their will to noble causes. There will be a glow on your face and a particular charm in your smile. You will possess a magnetic aura, which your friends will notice. You will be able to influence others. You will become an instrument of the Divine Will!

CHAPTER 12

DEVELOPING CONCENTRATION

When flowing loosely over a wide area, every force in nature moves more slowly and with less power than if gathered in one mass and directed through a single restricted outlet. Dammed and accumulated, the once sluggish and leisurely flow of a river rushes out with amazing force through the sluice. The warm rays of the sun focused through a magnifying glass become hot enough to burn objects. Such is the power generated by the concentration of force.

Swami Vishnudevananda

By harnessing the dissipated rays of our mind, we can bring it under our control, and make it work as we would like it and direct its energies as we wish. Whosoever has learned the science of concentration will understand the secrets of nature. There is no limit to the power of the human mind; the more concentrated it is, the more power it has.

Each one of us has a capacity for sustained attention; people of great intelligence or memory owe their gifts to being able to concentrate for long periods of time. All creativity, originality, knowledge, discovery and insight arise from concentration. A scientist, through the practice of concentration, opens layer upon layer of his or her mind and penetrates deeply into its higher regions bringing forth knowledge. The distracted mind has no access to its own creative potential. We live in times when the very way of life is such that sustained focus is discouraged. Due to the speed of technology and other factors including poor quality of food and education, there is a decline of mental capacity and mental health within the population. We are witnessing the shortening of the attention span throughout the population, particularly in children and it is happening at an alarming rate. Problems such as poor memory, inability to concentrate, restlessness, drug and substance abuse, and other mental disorders have developed as a result.

Remember that memory, will power, power of attention or more specifically, concentration are all closely-interrelated mental functions. If we develop good attentive power and power of concentration, memory and will power automatically increase. The two common mental extremes—attention deficit (when our mind is passive and scattered) and hyperactivity (when our mind is overactive)—are not confined only to those who are diagnosed with such conditions. These disturbances are symptoms of every unbalanced mind. Hyperactivity, characterized by distraction, excitation and agitation, is often accompanied by a host of negative emotions including anger, irritability and anxiety, while attention deficit manifests as negligence, dullness and lethargy.

In order to gauge just how challenging the process of concentration has become, think for a moment about the effect that modern media and the internet has on our minds. From the minute we turn on our screens, a constant stream of information, sounds and images assaults our senses and destroys our ability to focus. We cannot read or watch the news peacefully without constant interruption from an overdose of unwanted and unrequested information. It is easy to see how detrimental this is for our mental wellbeing. We can sustain only very short periods of concentration, causing stress and other mental issues. It seems nowadays that we are not supposed to concentrate for any length of time! Look at the role of advertising in our daily lives. Next time you are on your phone or computer take a serious look at the advertisements with which we are constantly bombarded and that have nothing or very little to do with the content of what we are reading. Watching television has become an increasingly stressful activity filled with distractions of all kinds. As the speed of technology steadily increases, in equal measure our attention span decreases. If we watch a movie that is ten or more years old we wait impatiently for a particular scene to end and a new one to begin. We are fed shorter and shorter film clips and faster and faster sound bites. Films and advertisements have become a strange mix of sound and light effects that are intended more to stun the mind than to nourish it.

Let us look at the subject of concentration from the yogic point of view.

Desha-bandhash-cittasya dharana—Concentration is holding the mind to one form or object steadily for a long time.

Yoga Sutras, III-1

Concentration is centering the mind steadily on a single thought or idea to the exclusion of all others. Concentration culminates in the experience of meditation in which the subject and the object of concentration merge into one; where there is no awareness of the external environment. We practice concentration to stop the mental modifications of the mind. Real spiritual progress is born from a state of concentration.

We have all had the experience of being engrossed in a book, oblivious to the sounds around us or the wafting aroma of a delicious meal close by; in fact with no sense impressions of our immediate environment. When we experience true concentration the senses are quiet and we experience a form of bliss. When we meet a friend whom we have not seen for a long time, the actual happiness we feel does not arise from the person as such, although it may seem so, but from within ourselves. We experience happiness as the result of our mind having become focused. In the absence of all other thoughts we concentrate, and continue to do so, on the very feeling of happiness. Similarly, when we enjoy a beautiful scene in nature it is the concentration and the attention that give us pleasure.

However the mind in its very nature is restless like the wind. Its restlessness can be compared to a monkey jumping from branch to branch, drunk and with a gun in its hand! A dangerous combination indeed! We can also compare the mind to a wild elephant let loose in a crowded market. Through the power of association, one single thought in the mind leads to an infinite number of other thoughts and we drift aimlessly away. How often is our mind elsewhere during a conversation? Although the senses are present, the connecting power—the mind—is absent.

On a conscious level, the mind appears to carry out several functions simultaneously, but in reality it can think of only one thing at a time. It moves with lightning speed from thought to thought, from one sense impression to another, from one object to another, and seems to do several things at the same time. However it is simply switching at break-neck speed between the tasks or perceptions. For perception to take place, the mind has to be connected to the senses through the eyes, ears, mouth, skin and nose. When the mind is attending to one thing, such as hearing a sound, for that brief moment it does not consciously experience any other sensation, object or thought. The key here is conscious thought. If for example, the perception is related to seeing, then, while seeing, the mind does not hear. Although the mind seems to be doing two actions—hearing and seeing—what really happens is that the subconscious mind takes over the first activity, that of hearing, while the conscious mind is seeing. Thus the mind builds a sense of false reality, that of multitasking.

The practice of developing attention (*avadhaana*) is to be mastered before we can embark on developing concentration. It is through the power of attention that the mind carries out its activities. Attention means to attend to or to perceive an object. We can only perceive if attention is involved. It is less specific than concentration. Concentration signifies the narrowing of the field of attention to a smaller circle. Attention is the basis of willpower and plays an important role in concentration. When attention is properly directed toward the inner recesses of our mind for the purpose of deep introspection, the light of awareness illumines the mind, allowing us to analyze its content and powers. In higher states of concentration, with the help of such attention—knowledge of any field, of the mind itself, or the universe—is disclosed. It is through attention that we gain clear knowledge of an object.

The force wherewith anything strikes the mind is generally in proportion to the degree of attention bestowed upon it. Moreover, the great art of memory is attention and inattentive people have bad memories. Power of attention becomes weakened in old age.

Swami Sivananda

Attention and concentration should pervade all aspects of your life. Here are some guidelines for approaching every action you do:

- For the attainment of one-pointedness we need purity of mind. We must develop a strong moral and ethical foundation, and in addition practice yoga asanas (*asana*) and breathing exercises (*pranayama*). The practice of virtues purifies the mind; the practice of asana and pranayama purifies and steadies the mind.

- Attention may be directed subjectively or internally on an idea or objectively or externally on an object. A well-trained mind can fix at will on any object, either inwardly or outwardly.

- Notice the quality of your ability to be attentive; whether you are steady or wavering. Observe the degree and duration, the level of fluctuation and the distractions that arise. Every time you notice the mind wandering off gently bring it back to the object of concentration. Develop the ability to handle distractions and return to the task at hand. Do not get side-tracked. Maintain fluidity. If you find the mind is losing its focus and beginning to wander, try to arouse your attention by will or create interest by using autosuggestion.

- Concentration and relaxation go hand-in-hand. Stay relaxed, still and vigilant. Stillness of the body helps to settle the mind.

- Interest develops attention; attention allows impressions to be imprinted deeply in the mind.

- Do not live aimlessly. Have a goal and a plan for your practice. Destroy aimless thinking; abandon 'building castles in the air.'

- Buddha said, "When you walk, walk! When you talk, talk! But do not wobble!" Do one thing at a time, and do it well.

- Avoid working in a haphazard way; work systematically and let your actions flow and your movements be graceful.

- Avoid hasty conclusions or making a big issue out of something small.

- Restlessness of the mind can be removed by breathing exercises. If the mind is restless and your thoughts start to run wild, relax by concentrating on deep breathing.

- Focus your entire attention on whatever you are doing at the moment. Live in the present.

- It is easy to concentrate the mind on an object which the mind likes. Practice concentrating on unpleasant tasks, people and situations. Keep their image before your mind's eye and interest will slowly develop. Many mental weaknesses such as worry, fear or irritability will gradually decrease and the mind will strengthen.

- Write a list of activities that you do daily but perhaps with little awareness or love. Attention, interest and love foster concentration. Bring your heart into all that you do. For example, would you like to be more focused in how you eat? Ask yourself, "How do I eat? Do I eat slowly with awareness or too fast?"

- Choose one task and do it with the utmost attention and with as much gentleness as possible. You will find fulfillment in the work itself rather than in the results alone. Gradually increase this practice to five actions, and then to ten.

- Concentration increases by lessening the number of desires.

Do not allow the mind to dissipate its energy on useless thoughts, worthless worry, useless imagination and fear. Hold the mind on one thought-form for half an hour by incessant practice.

Swami Sivananda

Initially we have to make a conscious effort to develop an attentive and concentrated mind and there may be resistance. But once the mind becomes focused we experience great joy and happiness. Train the mind in a variety of ways in the beginning. Due to its externalizing tendency, the mind can easily concentrate on external objects. Concentrate on the blue sky, sunrise, sun, moon or stars or on any concrete image. Concentrate on your natural breath, or on coordinating your breath with the repetition of a mantra such as *Om, So'ham* or your personal mantra. Then as the mind strengthens bring the concentration inside and focus on such objects as the chakras of the body, or as you advance on abstract ideas such as truth and love. Concentrate on the third eye, the space between the two eyebrows—the seat of the mind in the waking state. By concentrating here you can easily control the mind. Those who are more devotional in nature can concentrate on the heart, the seat of emotion and feeling.

The benefits of the practice of concentration are immense. Your memory as well as your will power will improve. You will develop penetrative insight. You will have the ability to visualize objects clearly even in their absence. You will have more time and you will always feel fresh and energized. You will not be tormented by the passage of time. You will remain young, calm and joyful. Concentration purifies the mind of surging emotions, strengthens the current of thought and clarifies ideas.

EXERCISE I
TRATAK (CANDLE-GAZING)

Tratak or gazing is a traditional exercise used to improve concentration. It is usually followed by mental visualization of the same image at the third eye. Gaze on a symbol such as Om, a black dot, an image of a saint, something in nature or on a candle. It is better to choose an uplifting image. Practice candle-gazing in a dark room free from any draft. Sit in a comfortable cross-legged position with the back straight with the candle burning steadily, placed with flame at eye-level and at arm's distance. Take a few deep breaths and relax. Now open the eyes wide. Gaze at the flame for one minute, keeping the eyes open. Try not to blink but avoid straining the eyes. After one minute close the eyes and visualize the flame at the point between the eyebrows. Again and again gently conjure up the image. Continue with the visualization for one minute. With practice lengthen the time of gazing and visualization to two minutes and eventually to five.

EXERCISE 2
FOCUSED READING

Read one or two of pages of a book. As you read let go of any distracting thoughts and focus exclusively on the matter in hand. Read slowly and attentively, allowing the mind to bring together, classify, group and compare. You will gain a tremendous amount of understanding and knowledge from your reading. Oftentimes we skim and skip, with no awareness of doing so, and as a consequence have little recollection of what we have read.

EXERCISE 3
THE SOUND OF OM

Sit by the sea where you can hear the waves dashing against the shore, or by a river. With deep concentration the sound you will hear will be the sound *Om*. Concentrate on this sound for as long as you can. This practice is very uplifting and expands the mind.

CHAPTER 13

THE PRACTICE OF MEDITATION

The happiest moments are the ones when thought ceases. All happiness is simply the absence of thought. It is timelessness itself. Meditation and non-reacting (non-attachment) are the way to this happiness. All beings search for happiness. The search never stops. But happiness does not lie outside, as commonly imagined, but within each one of us. What is at the core behind our incessant pursuit for happiness is the fact that happiness is our intrinsic nature. It is who we are. And we will never stop until we find it. What we are really looking for is already there; it is with us and within us, but in our ignorance we believe that happiness is to be found in time and space. And each time we arrive at what we thought was happiness, we never actually find it and so we move on, readying ourselves for another possibility. In reality happiness is an experience beyond time and space. True happiness lies beyond thought in the realm of what we may call Awareness, or Inner Silence. We are continuously trying to regain the lost paradise but the paradise was never lost. It is only imagined so.

Our external conditions are important for contentment and happiness, no doubt, but they do not, by themselves, bring about this experience. If that were the case then the most fortunate of human beings would have found permanent happiness. We must make a distinction between pleasure, which is the experience of temporary happiness, and the experience of true happiness as the expression of our deeper nature, found only in those who have gained wisdom.

Take the example of a person playing golf who mistakes the pleasure of a successful game as true happiness. Most of us imagine that the experience of happiness arises when we accomplish a task, succeed in something, or possess something. We think happiness is simply sensory excitement; and as a resultthe search for happiness turns into a psychological dependence on something outside of us. However, the secret of happiness is to stop searching outside; it is to reduce the number of thoughts through the process of concentration which reaches its climax when there is a complete absence of thought and we rest in our true nature as Pure Being. We must learn to understand the mind—consciously and steadily reducing all unnecessary thought—and live in the moment.

Life is nothing but an interplay of thoughts. Our world is experienced as the world of duality. Duality ceases when our mind stops. Only when we reach into the depths of our mind will we be able to find peace. It is when thought comes to stillness—such as in deep meditation—that the power of the inner Self or Awareness surges forth. Thinking therefore must cease. Make it a point daily to go deep within to the place that knows no stress, tension, duality. Then and there alone will you attain timeless Awareness.

True happiness is beyond thought; it arises when thoughts are absent. The greatest bliss commonly known to most people is the happiness of deep sleep. Many of us are searching outside in vain for the experience of happiness hoping that one day it will come to stay. We don't know that true happiness comes from within. It does not come in time since it does not belong to time. It is beyond time.

Happiness is most sweetly found in the precious moments when the mind is free from thought. To access it learn to step out of your thoughts and just be, remaining still. It is in that Being, in that absence of thought that happiness is found as the most natural experience.

We have all tried to make this world an abode of permanent happiness through the pursuit of pleasure. We have all felt that the world owes us something and if only we knew where to look for it and find it, everything would be all right. But we have failed—not only you and me, but everyone. Why? Because we have miscalculated our purpose in life.

The various experiences of suffering that we have all had from our search for permanent happiness outside, show us that the world cannot give us what is not there. There is no permanent happiness in the world. It is bereft of true happiness. How can something essentially transitory, unstable and changing give us that which is stable and permanent? The spiritual teachings are clear—change your outlook on the world! The world and our life are nothing but a school, a training ground where we have come to learn many useful lessons. This world is where we discipline our body and mind and develop our capacities to the fullest. This is where we learn to share our gifts with others, learn to sacrifice for others and to love all. The happiest moments are the ones when thought ceases. All happiness is simply the absence of thoughts. It is timelessness itself.

Just as the light is burning within an enclosed lamp, so also is the divine flame burning from time immemorial in the lamp of your heart. Close your eyes. Merge yourself within the divine flame. Plunge deep into the chambers of your heart. Meditate on this divine flame and become one with the flame of God.

Swami Sivananda

Meditation is the consummation of the spiritual path. It stands for the realization of our ultimate purpose of life. Meditation is a grand house that is built on strong foundations (*yamas and niyamas*) without which it will not stand. We look for happiness outside of ourselves, but happiness is the experience that manifests from within. Concentration brings stillness to the mind and the happiness within is then experienced. Meditation as a practice cultivates this inner experience.

Tatra pratyayaikataanataa dhyaannam—a continuous flow of perceptions (or thoughts) is meditation (dhyana).

Yoga Sutras III-2

Meditation is an experience which cannot be described. We cannot determine at what point we have entered into meditation, as with sleep. Meditation is a transcendental experience. To transcend means to go beyond or cross over. It is the experience of timeless, spaceless, causeless reality, beyond speech, senses and intellect—the experience of the true Self.

According to the teachings of Yoga and Vedanta, there are four states of consciousness:

1. Waking
2. Dream
3. Deep sleep
4. *Turīya* (superconscious state; the state of meditation)

In the wakeful state, our senses and intellect operate. We are aware of the world around us. There is a distinct sense of the existence of oneself as subject and other as object. In the dream state our mind creates a reality of its own from the impressions received in the waking state. In our dreams the subtle senses are active and we see, hear and experience different emotions. The mind divides itself into subject and object. Objects appear to have an existence of their own but in fact the subject creates them. In deep sleep there is no mental activity; complete rest follows the cessation of thinking and neither subject nor object exist. Here there are no sense-impressions; the mind is temporarily merged or dissolved in consciousness. There is awareness of neither time nor space, no subject/object relationship. We experience bliss but are not aware of it until we awaken. We 'remember' deep sleep as an experience full of bliss. The fourth state, *turīya* is beyond the other three and is also known as *samadhi* or the superconscious state. Here there is no time, space, mind nor world—only full of awareness of the pure *I AM* in the eternal now.

What is meditation? It is the experience of timelessness, infinity and causelessness. Our true nature as Pure Existence (Being)—that which is beyond time and space—has no cause. It exists beyond cause and effect. There are many meditation techniques. Meditation generally involves concentration on some uplifting image and/or a repetition of a sacred name of the Lord or mantras. Once the mind is sufficiently quiet, achieved by steadying the mind and focusing on the breath, we concentrate on an uplifting image or mantra.

Mantras have been used for thousands of years as a means to reach the highest perfection. A mantra carries a special energy within its sound vibrations. *Japa* is the repetition of a mantra and its practice removes the impurities of the mind. On repetition of a mantra the mind is lifted from the ordinary state of consciousness to the telepathic and ultimately to the transcendental state of meditation. Its pure energy lifts the mind from its lowest level to its highest level, that of pure thought. In the fourth stage of consciousness, name, form and our own Self as witness are indistinguishable. The mantra acts as a ladder to take us beyond the mind. The mantras used are in Sanskrit, considered to be the oldest language in the world, with its structure and sound vibrations linked to the root energies that lie behind creation. It is a language that is closely related to the highest states of consciousness. The word mantra itself comes from two Sanskrit verbal roots: *man* meaning to think, and *tra* from trai meaning to protect, or to free. From the root *man* we get the word 'man' (a being that thinks).

A mantra is mystical energy encased in a sound structure, or in simple language—energy that is contained within a special sound.

Swami Vishnudevananda

A mantra generates the creative force and bestows eternal Bliss. A mantra when constantly repeated awakens the consciousness.

Swami Sivananda

Every mantra contains within its vibrations a certain power. When we concentrate and repeat a mantra its energy is elicited and takes form. Mantras were first discovered by *rishis*, (seers who were in *samadhi*). As they were coming out of the deepest state of consciousness they perceived an energy—like a thread—as they came down to the ordinary state of consciousness. When that energy, connecting the highest state of consciousness with the ordinary state, became more defined, it took the form of these sacred sounds. By following this energy the rishis were able to re-enter the superconscious state. Those who discovered or saw the mantras were called *drashtas* (the seers of the mantras). Mantras are energies that have always existed in the universe. Just as the law of gravity was not invented but discovered by Isaac Newton, so also the rishis discovered these subtle energies; they did not invent them. Different mantras were discovered by different rishis.

On repetition of a mantra the mind is lifted from the ordinary state of consciousness to the telepathic and ultimately to the transcendental state of meditation. The mantra acts as a ladder to take us beyond the mind. Its pure energy lifts the mind from its lowest level to its highest level, that of pure thought. In the fourth stage of consciousness, name, form and our own Self as witness are indistinguishable.

The following are some commonly used mantras:

OM ŚRĪ MAHĀ GAṆAPATAYE NAMAḤ

OM NAMAḤ ŚIVĀYA

OM NAMO NĀRĀYAṆĀYA

OM NAMO BHAGAVATE VĀSUDEVĀYA

OM ŚRĪ RĀMĀYA NAMAḤ

OM ŚRĪ DURGĀYAI NAMAḤ

OM ŚRĪ MAHĀ LAKṢMYAI NAMAḤ

OM ŚRĪ SARASVATYAI NAMAḤ

OM

SO'HAM

Principles of the practice of meditation:

- For those new to the practice it is preferable to keep a regular time and place for your practice.

- It is when thought comes to stillness in deep meditation that the power of the inner Self or Awareness surges forth. Make it a point daily to go to the place within that knows no stress, tension or duality. Build a routine. Meditate every day, regardless of the results or the state of your mind. If you miss even one day in your practice you will feel a great loss, as if your mind has not received proper nourishment.

- Establish the ideal time for your practice. The best time for meditative practice is before sunrise, 4-6am (*brahmamuhurta*), sunset, or at night. During brahmamuhurta the mind is clear and peaceful. As there are no impressions from the previous day, the mind is like a blank piece of paper on which we can write new, positive impressions. The first impressions of the day are the most important as they mold our mind's response to the day's events. At this time the quality of sattva (pure energy) operates at its highest level. The psychic channel in our energy body, called *sushumna*, is open. Night removes the idea of multiplicity of objects which are normally visible in the daylight; darkness facilitates the arising of the sense of unity.

- Set up your meditation space. Space is a living entity and retains energy from the activities and the thoughts of those within it. As you continue to meditate your space will generate a healing and relaxing energy. The subtle vibrations from your practice will be imprinted in its atmosphere. During times of stress you can simply sit and feel the restorative energy of the space charged by your meditative practice. Every place is associated with the action performed within it. For example in the kitchen, we tend to think of food. Even if we are not hungry we open the fridge —habitual! Your meditation space is an energy-container for your practice.

- Create a focus—a mini, sacred altar on which you can put a few uplifting symbols such as images, statues, flowers or small oil lamp—anything that inspires and uplifts you. Light symbolises the element of fire as well as the light of knowledge or the light of awareness. In the presence of fire (or flame) thoughts are amplified and serve as a means of communication between the physical world and the higher astral realms. Light purifies the energy of a room.

- Burn incense, which purifies the air and uplifts the mind (sandalwood and frankincense are preferred).

- Develop harmony and integrity of personality. Increase pure thoughts in your mind. Strive to live a life without contradiction. Endeavour to make all aspects of life sattvic (pure). Make everything you do—talking, eating, listening, thinking, studying, keeping company and even dressing—a reflection of a higher and purer quality of the mind.

- Cultivate non-attachment.

Practical Steps to Meditation:

1) Sit cross-legged on the floor, on a mat or cushion if possible. Sit straight, but with no tension. Sitting cross-legged preserves the energy within the body. The triangular formation of the body resembles a pyramid—the triangular structure of a pyramid is known to be the best way to keep energy circulating within. Our energy dissipates mainly through the feet and hands and the top of the head.

2) Place the hands in *chin-mudra* (by bringing the thumb and index finger on each hand together) with hands facing upwards. *Chit* means consciousness; *mudra* means seal or gesture. This positioning of the hands represents the union of individual consciousness with cosmic consciousness. The thumb represents the supreme or cosmic consciousness, also called *paramaatman*; the index finger represents the ego and psychically has a negative energy; the other three fingers represent the three gunas (qualities of nature).

3) Regulate the breathing by inhaling for three seconds and exhaling for three seconds. This allows all mental and physical activity to quieten. Then slow down your breath to a comfortable rate.

4) Now choose a focal point, either the point between the eyes or the heart center (in the middle of the chest).

5) Start coordinating the repetition of the mantra *Om* or any sacred mantra with the inhalation and exhalation of the breath.

6) Listen to the sound of the mantra.

7) Whenever a thought or a sound distracts the mind, simply recognize the distraction without identifying with it. Let it go and come back to the mantra. Do not use force to control your mind, but rather understanding and patience. There should be no strain in the practice of meditation.

8) Gradually the awareness of the breath will fade out and only awareness will shine. The mantra, the person who repeats it and the process of the repetition of the mantra will merge into one consciousness.

The benefits of the practice of meditation are manifold. The fire of meditation awakens the intuitive faculty and makes the mind calm and steady. All doubts gradually clear. A mysterious inner voice will guide you. You will feel inner strength, new vigor and vitality. Meditation develops a powerful mind. The positive vibrations created by the practice of meditation act on all the cells of the body, bringing harmony and health to all organs. If you meditate for half an hour every day you will face all the temptations and challenges of daily life with calmness, patience and wisdom. You will develop a magnetic and charming personality and have a positive influence on many people; they will derive joy and peace in your presence. Meditation cuts the knot of egoism and ignorance. It is the only way to Self-realization or Self-Knowledge or God.

CHAPTER 14

WITNESSING

I give you a secret very profound. The mind is everything. To take the moment and find the chance to turn inwards and watch your own thoughts, to be aware of your own thoughts while you are in a witnessing mood is the greatest hour of earthly joy.

Swami Sivananda

To know that the universe is objectified thought and that one is the Awareness beyond is the pinnacle of all spiritual teachings. To realize that all our joys and sorrows, circumstances and experiences including the smallest detail are nothing but the thoughts of past and future manifested, and that there is only Pure Consciousness—this is to know. Until we are able to reach the Awareness behind the curtain of thoughts, the mind needs to be trained to remain silent. Let all the waves of thought subside. In that stillness, when the mind melts, there shines the self-effulgent Atman, Pure Consciousness. Watch the mind. Watch the thoughts. Pursue serenity. It is towards this great Stillness that we all gravitate. The Reality is reached only when all thoughts subside. It is only then that the real You emerges. The inner Self is the repository of all goodness, love, wisdom and compassion. Mastery over and transcendence of thought is indeed the purpose of life. To be able to disassociate from our thoughts is the fundamental step and the most important discovery of our life. It is the beginning of the conquest of the mind, of the breaking of samsara (the cycle of birth and death). There is no happiness, no peace, no spiritual experience, until we are able to detach from the endless stream of thought.

The state of witnessing is not an uncommon experience. When we gaze out of a window at home or when travelling, we are in the state of witnessing. When we feel happiness as we survey nature in her pristine glory from a mountain top we are in the state of witnessing and it is this state that brings us happiness.

To understand the technique of witnessing we have to become aware of how we identify with our thoughts. When a thought arises in the mind, we have a choice—we either identify with it, or we let it pass. Ordinarily we identify with them, as well as our bodies and emotions. To identify with something means to assume or take on the qualities of an object, qualities that are not originally ours. The word 'identification' is derived from the Latin word idem, meaning 'same' and the verb *facere*, 'to make'. To identify is to make something the same. In this context, it appears as if the 'I', or the sense of one's Self, or the Awareness which by its very presence knows the thought, takes on the qualities of the particular thought, the qualities which do not intrinsically belong to it.

We say, "I am angry," or "I am happy," imputing the sense of I and mine onto the feeling. However there is clearly a differentiation between the subject, me, and the object, the feeling. Awareness, which by its nature shines on its own, is always separate from the thought. Yet when we identify with the thought, the Awareness seems to take on the qualities of the thought. That which is aware of the thought, and yet is not the thought, and that which precedes the arising of the thought and continues to exist even after the thought has ceased to exist, is the Awareness, our true Self. Therefore identification is not a real process but takes place only in appearance. There cannot be a relationship between the unchanging Awareness and the changing thoughts, just as there cannot be a relationship between the light projected during the movie and the screen onto which it is projected. This process extends via thought to every possible object that we identify with in this world. As we endow each one of them with a sense of self, they become me! Identification with a thought generally causes more thoughts of a similar nature to manifest in the mind. To avert this constant and neverending habit, initially we simply observe the mind. When we observe the mind, it quietens. When left to run about unnoticed it brings in a host of negative thoughts—worries and thoughts of dejection. It is only when we invest interest in a particular thought or a state of mind that we are at their mercy. Learn to witness and let the mind settle in silence.

The Self, or Awareness is. Awareness is simply being, as opposed to becoming (thinking). Thoughts change whereas Awareness remains unmodified by any thought. Awareness is the eternal witness; it is a changeless witness of the ever-changeful mind. Awareness is never an object of perception. In the practice of witnessing, we remain still amidst the interferences and demands of the inner and outer world.

To witness means to observe or have a clear awareness of what actually happens *to* us and *in* us, at each successive moment of perception, without reacting to it by deed, speech or mental comment. If a reaction takes place then we are to witness it as another thought. We observe the play of life as though we are watching a movie but without identification. The process entails introspection and close awareness of the mental waves. We witness the arising of thoughts as well as their absence. The witnessing consciousness exists regardless of whether there are thoughts or not. Every act of witnessing is an act of transcendence; it allows us to rise above a thought or emotion and have a broader vision. Whatever we identify with has a certain power over us and controls our life. Whenever we identify with a thought we make it stronger and it magnifies its hold on us. In the process of witnessing, a thought or sensation is under the observation of the witnessing consciousness or Awareness. We cease to be involved with our reactions.

Additional principles in the practice of witnessing are as follows:

- Practice witnessing daily for at least a few minutes. Ask yourself frequently, "What am I thinking about?"

- To understand your mind you need to watch it all the time. Train yourself to 'ride' with unpleasant feelings and thoughts without letting yourself be affected by them. Watch the mind when it fears or when a desire or anger takes hold of it.

- Practice thought-stopping or thought-inhibition from time to time.

- Never allow the mind to be completely extrovert and absorbed in the objects of the world.

- Don't fight the thoughts. Don't force the silence or peace. Let thoughts be.

- Do not give assent to the suggestions made by thoughts.

- Do not own your thoughts. The concern and the fighting give them life! Cease to nourish especially-negative thoughts by dwelling on them.

The general rule in witnessing is to give no more attention or emphasis to thoughts than is needed. There are two stages to the process:

I. ***Witness sensory perceptions.*** Concentrate on external sounds such as noise or visual forms without regarding them as disturbances. Do not react to what you hear or see.

2. *Witness thought processes* such as planning, imagining, ruminating. Maintain the following attitude: "I am not involved in this thought or this thinking process; I am just watching it happen. The thoughts and sensations come and go. They are not always present. But as a witness I am always present." Instead of saying, "I am upset or I am happy," say, "Upset is in the mind; happiness is in the mind. I am just the witness, the witness of the mind." With awareness such emotions will eventually lose their strength, and you will be able to handle them safely.

As the light reveals all the objects remaining in its own place, so the witness-consciousness, itself ever motionless, illumines the objects within and without.

Panchadasi

To be established in the sublime state of witnessing is to find our true freedom. As long we identify with our thoughts and emotions believing them to have the exclusive reality, we perpetuate our bondage and are enslaved by the very thoughts we think. The only factor that truly controls our life is this process of identification. We do not need to cease thinking or feeling; we simply need to know that we are not what we think and what we feel; we are that which transcends the thinking subject and the thoughts as objects—we are Life, Consciousness itself.

CHAPTER 15

SELF-EMPOWERMENT

Every one of you is a power in yourself. You can influence others. You can radiate Joy and Peace to millions upon millions of people far and near. You can elevate others even from a long distance. You can transmit your powerful, soul-stirring, beneficial thoughts to others, because you are an image of God, nay, you are God Himself the moment the veil of ignorance enshrouding you is rent asunder.

Swami Sivananda

Most of us have been brainwashed into thinking that we are not important and that we have no power of our own. Power seems to belong to everyone but ourselves. Our first duty is to resuscitate ourselves from within. We must learn to trust the strength, the resourcefulness, the skill and the capacity that lie within us. True education awakens our lion-like spirit; its goal is not to make us into spiritless money-making machines.

A significant step towards freedom comes when we realize that all events, people, conditions and the seemingly most trivial occurrences, are determined by the state of our mind, by our most cherished and deepest thoughts.

To change our quality of thought requires sincerity, consistent effort and discipline. For lifetimes we have allowed different 'weeds' to grow in the mind. Now the task to remove them looks stupendous. But don't despair! The goal is to rise above all thoughts and rest in the radiance of joy and the glow of wisdom that are our very essence.

The remedy for any problem, individually and collectively, lies in utilizing the power of choice in the cultivation of right thought. Self-reliance rests on this principle alone. Self-effort is a gift to be rediscovered moment by moment. There is no friend or enemy outside of us. All benevolence springs from within only. Therefore cherish your good thoughts and let them act as a guardian of the treasury.

We live in a world that we have created for ourselves out of our own thoughts. Our world is continually in the making. It is consciously being reshaped and redesigned through the power of our mind. Our world has no name or designation; it is not on anyone's map. It is made up of everything that we have ever thought and lived. It is being molded at every moment by each one of our choices, thoughts, feelings and imaginations; we see the world outside only relative to the quality of our own world inside. Our perception of the world is nothing but the reflection of our world within. Our mind is like an artist and the world we see is the canvas; how our world looks is determined by our skill as a painter and the kind of colors we use. As long as we continue to think the same thoughts, to have the same opinions, the world we live in will remain the same. State bravely, "I have the power to free myself from all falseness and ignorance. I will create a better world for all."

Therefore . . . strive, strive, strive. Strive when the darkness overwhelms your heart, continue to strive when the first light breaks through, and continue to strive even at the peak, at the summit of your life. It is striving that makes you a hero. It is endeavor and practice that are the cause of your excellence, and it is the same striving that is the measure of your life. Striving and love go together. Striving is love's call to the ultimate goal. At the end of your life there will be perhaps only two questions you will have to answer: How hard did you strive? and How deep was your love? Shatter all fear and anger; cast out worry and distrust. Remember to keep the flame of inspiration forever alive. It is inspiration that awakens your spirit's energy and brings you to the height of your being. Let the spark of your inspiration become the flame of your realization. Open your heart to inspiration; draw inspiration from all directions. The effort must be yours, there can be no substitute. You can be shown the steps, but it is only you who can walk them. No one can save you but yourself. Just as no one can eat for you, exercise or meditate for you, so too you must understand that your own effort is the greatest blessing and boon!

Remember that time is limited. Time is the ever-decreasing, ever-changing credit with which we operate and it must be invested in the right pursuits. The tide of time has deceived many. Almost all but the most accomplished know that time is the one factor in life over which we have no control. When the time is up, we have to leave. Time is impartial; it makes no difference whether you are spiritual aspirant or business magnate. It spares no one. Our day is twenty-four hours and a year twelve months. As we move forward, time silently slips by. Each sunset, each day crossed off on the calendar is a reminder of the evanescent nature of time and of the greater efforts we must put into achievement of the great life-purpose and realization of our dream. We cannot afford to live in the illusion of permanency, missing precious opportunities and misdirecting our energy.

Life is full of beginnings. They are presented every day and every hour to every person. Most beginnings are small and appear trivial and insignificant, but in reality they are the most important things in life. Not only great happiness but great power arises from doing little things unselfishly, wisely, and perfectly, for life in its totality is made up of little things. Wisdom inheres in the common details of everyday existence.

James Allen

In whatever we want to accomplish, there must be a beginning. Life consists of new beginnings. Wisdom is acting on this knowledge. A right beginning precedes all change in the right direction. We can always start again, anew. This knowledge gives us new hope and joy. A new positive thought, a new initiative, a new action, a fresh approach, a new accomplishment. We are reborn every moment. It requires a positive and sustained effort to stop the mind dwelling on past mistakes. A spiritual aspirant believes only in the power of now, of the present moment. No more yesterday—always anew, each and every time. Living life in this manner is to practice a constant meditation in which we keep returning to the present moment, and reconnecting with our Inner Self or God. To be inspired we must learn to live every moment anew as if we were just born. What does it feel like to be born every moment into the stream of life and energy? There has to be a sense of freshness or newness in all actions we do—in our look, our words, our yoga practice, meditation, cooking—in each and every action!

The world is for your education. You learn several lessons daily. If you learn all you can, if you utilize all opportunities to the best advantage, in the spirit of yoga, then your capacities and willpower will develop. You grow, you evolve, you expand.

Swami Sivananda

Remember the lessons you are here to learn. They are the foundation of compassion for yourself and others. If you can remember the bruises from your falls, the pangs of desperation, the heavy darkness that have at times enveloped your soul, the painful consequences of bitter mistakes, the sting of reprimand from others, the inability to change how others thought of you, when you were left only with God's grace and time's healing hand, you will know what takes place in the heart of the struggling soul, and you will wish to see their agony melt away; you will gladly offer them the comfort of your love and strength.

The world's purpose is to give us the exact lessons we need—there may be lessons in love, acceptance, development of a skill, a philosophical lesson. Everything that the world has to offer has a relationship with a lesson for us to learn for the simple reason that we and the world are one and the same entity. At the end of each day, contemplate on all the lessons given and grow in wisdom.

Rightly used, rightly directed, the very means of fall are the means of rise.

Sanskrit proverb

There is no perfection in this world. Wherever we go, there is duality of condition—something beneficial and something challenging. In all circumstances we have to learn to create our own inner world, full of light. Mastery over the mind is the only remedy for all the ills of living. Until we have learned to transform the challenges we face into the means of growth, we have not yet started to live. The challenge of all challenges is how to integrate our challenges into the tools for our evolution.

An insightful look into the difficulties we face will show us that they never appear arbitrarily and that our so-called enemies are nothing but indispensable tools for our growth related to our innermost needs. Challenges that exist in forms such as obstacles, failures, impediments, problems, hurdles, tests and trials are inherent in creation and have an exact role to play in our life. They are simply part of the growth of the soul on its journey to the Infinite Reality. They are there as a means for us to evolve, but often lie beyond our ability to intuit.

Generally we feel that most of our challenges appear simply to annoy us and prevent us from enjoying or getting on with our lives; failures seem to try to weaken us, and the great tragedies in our lives threaten to crush us. The purpose of challenge is to rediscover our own strength. Obstacles are blessings in disguise; they are simply part of the grand plan. We need to approach them in an open and positive way. Understanding what role difficulties play in our life is fundamental to spiritual life and to having peace of mind. Difficulties inhere in all places, people and circumstance. In the very structure of action and life, difficulties are intrinsic. No progress, no unfoldment, no evolution can take place without difficulties. Without them there would be universal stagnation.

Whenever there arises a need within us to open up, to learn, to release blocked energy, to take a leap up to the next level of understanding, wisdom or love, life brings its own lessons in the form of challenges appropriate to what is to be learned. If there is a prominent weakness in our nature, the circumstances form in such a way that they force us to face it. Once we can see the effect it has on our life, we can transmute it into a tool for our growth. Such a weakness becomes our teacher; we turn it to our own good until it is conquered. Circumstances unfold both our weaknesses as well as our strengths. For example, as long as there is in us a strong tendency to anger we will experience circumstances in which anger will manifest; we may even look at every situation as a potential trigger for anger. The solution is to see each situation as an opportunity to develop the opposite feeling—patience, forgiveness and acceptance.

All challenges in life are brought about by the particular needs of the individual or society and therefore are absolutely necessary in our evolution. In order to effectively deal with any challenge that may arise, the first step we must take is not to look at it as a 'punishment from above' and feel victimized by it. All challenges serve us in our evolution and are given by the cosmic intelligence which is running to our rescue. They are in fact a part of the creative process. We learn how to solve and eventually outgrow them. Every experience is a lesson in our lives and is exactly what we need at that moment. It must be learned or it will be repeated. There are no mistakes. Obstacles and challenges are nature's way of strengthening us. Just as our muscles only build when working against an opposing force, so the will, devotion, purity and spiritual strength can only develop against the force of difficulties, challenges, trials and tests! Just like a plant that is subjected daily to weather conditions in order to grow vigorous and strike deep roots, so also we are given obstacles to become a sturdy and beautiful instrument for the reception of the Divine Light and Wisdom. The degree of the power or strength hidden within us is equivalent to the type of obstacle with which we are faced. Let fear and resistance go.

The lessons of life are mastered only when we are able to feel gratitude for them; when we have accepted the truth that the Divine hand is in the background, always guiding and teaching. We are set free when we feel that our inner being has been enriched by the experiences of life and that our understanding, love and strength have increased due to them. We come to peace with the hardships we have gone through. We don't blame anyone or anybody; rather, we feel grateful that the universe has been kind enough to have given us such precious lessons.

If you don't control your own mind, somebody or something else will control it for you.

Swami Vishnudevananda

Freedom is to take responsibility for our own life. To be free, we need to stop blaming others for our misfortunes. To feel a victim of life and to keep others hostage in our mind deprives us of divine light and intuition, and suppresses an enormous amount of psychic energy and willpower. Most of us are familiar with the feeling of being a victim. We believe the people in our lives and the circumstances in which we find ourselves are the cause of our unhappiness. Free yourself from the tendency

158

to look for the causes of your problems and your shortcomings in people and circumstance. Then set free all people in your life from the obligation that they owe *you* something in order for *you* to be happy. The ability to transform our lives lies precisely in freeing others from the prison we have built for them in our heart, from the obligation that they owe us something—an apology, a smile, a better life, or anything that may make us feel more secure and whole. Such an attitude prevents positive change, paralyzes our will and blocks our future potential. It is when we think that others need to compensate us for what they have done that we end up in the role of victim. To be a victim is to say, "I have no power of my own. Whatever I do, I come under the spell of another's will or action." It may feel right to hold another responsible for who and what we are, but it undermines our own strength and happiness. The truth lies in self-empowerment, in ridding ourselves of the mesmerizing spell created by the victim attitude. Claim your life today—in every situation, however insignificant! And let others be free! By offering them freedom we become free. No being is ever responsible for what we achieve. Whatever we experience is always in accordance with the quality of a particular thought or *karma*.

There is justice behind every experience. Even the smallest of our experiences does not escape the precise mathematics of the glorious intelligence that runs all life. Every experience we have is a reaction, a response of the forces of nature that operate on the principle of the unity of everything, whether good or bad—that of *karma*. Every experience is a teacher. If you consider a negative experience as a form of injustice done to you, you will not evolve. Your progress will come to a halt. The true meaning of justice can only be understood when we take responsibility for our lives and learn to take control of our mind. When we cease to feel victims, we start to rediscover the power that is intrinsically existent, everpresent within us. By thinking that others hold the key to our happiness, we surrender that power to them and a life of dependency, suffering, and perhaps even addiction ensues. In order to comprehend this law, we need to deepen our understanding. Be silent within. As the silence deepens, we start to understand the operation of the hidden laws behind life. Once we become attuned to that voice of truth within, we abandon the tendency to hold others responsible for what we go through. It is a freeing and liberating experience indeed!

So let us rise up to work and create the best conditions for our realization and for bringing heaven to earth. Move from the personal to the impersonal, from the individual to the cosmic, from owning to disowning, from attachment to detachment. Now you have made a great step towards taking the initiative for your own self-healing and your own enlightenment. The truth is that it is only ourselves that can make ourselves whole.

Our challenges serve to deepen our compassion for others. Is there anybody in this world who has not risen to the heights of mastery, success, and glory without failures, without having made mistakes? The realization that all beings are fallible in the course of evolution should be the foundation of our humility and compassion and deep love for others—our brothers and sisters who have not yet risen to the heights of spiritual purity and mastery. We may think of our past failures only in order to understand the causes and processes that led to them. To think of them beyond that is to keep strengthening their impact in the form of habit. We cannot overcome weaknesses while continually pondering over them. All love for others is kindled by first acknowledging the lessons we have had to learn in our own life. By knowing the depth of our own suffering and the enormous love that has emerged from it, we know and understand the suffering of others. By having known the depths of anguish of the Dark Night of the Soul, we will know and realize the true light of the sun of Awareness that eternally shines in us! What a wonderful thing life is!

Occasionally we are aware that an aspect of our morality or of our mental or physical health is deteriorating. However, if we do not heed the signs, if we slacken our efforts and become passive, or simply if we are not able to solve the problem as we are not yet ready to mend our ways, suffering comes as a last resort to teach us. This suffering can bring about a major transformation and if we are sensitive enough we will see the kindness of the cosmic forces behind every experience of suffering.

Mastery in any field, and specifically in that of the spiritual, comes only with a price. Life is a school with an examination system by which we are constantly tested, moving from one grade to another, sometimes to a higher and at other times to a lower one. Life is an opportunity given to those who are courageous. The higher we want to go, the greater the obstacles, the greater the resistance from nature and the greater the price involved. The challenges come in different forms—in the form of tests of our strength, discrimination, selflessness, devotion and detachment from our body-consciousness. They come in the form of temptations manifested in proportion to our lack of mastery over desires, either physical or psychic, such as lust, anger, self-pride, fear, psychic experiences and powers and more—the list is long.

Our strength is measured against temptation. Temptation or desire is like gravity and the power of our insight is like a muscle. The stronger the insight and the will, the greater our ability is to lift ourselves and the greater our freedom. Our evolution is measured by the degree of mastery over temptations, desires and negative thinking that bind the soul. A temptation is nothing but an unconquered desire. And every desire will eventually be known and understood to have been illusory.

Every time you face a difficulty look at it as a gift, perhaps wrapped in a way that is not yet recognizable. Every difficulty is a calling for true strength and a solution. Strength is part of the solution. Spiritual heroes march on! Keep your heart open and take shelter in your most noble thoughts. Life has meaning only in striving. Celebrate every effort however tiny, every struggle however painful, every victory however small and every fall that leads you to the Light. Meditate daily, "I embrace all life, all experiences. I learn from everything and everyone. The whole universe is my supreme teacher. Every mistake I have ever made, every difficulty that I have ever faced was the manifestation of the greatest kindness of my guru in the form of life itself."

CHAPTER 16

A GARLAND OF VIRTUES

Think not lightly of evil, saying, 'It will not come to me.' Drop by drop is a water pot filled; likewise, the fool, gathering it little by little, fills himself with evil. Think not lightly of good, saying, 'It will not come to me.' Drop by drop is a water pot filled; likewise, the wise person, gathering it little by little, fills himself with good.

Buddha

It is challenging to be able to 'walk one's talk.' We are immersed in our imaginings of virtuousness but are unaware of how little accord there is between our thought and our actions. There is a 'disconnect' and lack of integrity in the hearts of most of us—the reason why so many spiritual seekers fall short of their ideals. For example, we may have a thought of kindness, but how present is that quality in our nature? Is it five percent or ninety percent? This is where the importance of self-analysis, keeping of a spiritual diary and an active, deliberate practice of virtues lies. Let your life speak more and more, and let your words fall silent. Then the true beauty of your spiritual heart will shine alone.

In spite of our many joyful moments, if we carefully analyze our earthly existence, we see that our lives are stained and permeated by disappointments both big and small, by suffering, mild and intense, and at times by the bitter experience of our illusions crashing, like the thunderous destruction of an iceberg. Despite our short-lived physical existence there is yet a grand purpose that we are to realize—that of the Oneness of all life. Life is a teacher par excellence!

Take up a virtue and develop it to its maximum. First familiarize yourself with its essential qualities, practices and the possible distractions that may arise in the practice. Meditate on the virtue before you start the practice and then keep a diary to see how often you have managed to implement it or failed. Practice the qualities below on a monthly basis. Make a commitment or a vow to sustain the practice for a certain amount of time by allocating a specific number of minutes or hours per day.

If you think of the opposite of fear, viz., courage, fear will slowly vanish. Have the word-image OM COURAGE before the mind. Repeat this formula often. A word is the center of an idea; an idea is the center of a mental image; a mental image is the center of a mental habit; a mental habit is the center of a trait in person. Have a clear-cut image in the mind of the quality of courage, and this quality will develop. The subconscious mind will do everything for you. The will also will come to your aid. Desire to be courageous, and the will will immediately follow desire.

Swami Sivananda

MEDITATION ON TWELVE VIRTUES
BY SWAMI SIVANANDA

HUMILITY in January
FRANKNESS in February
COURAGE in March
PATIENCE in April
MERCY in May
MAGNANIMITY in June
SINCERITY in July
PURE LOVE in August
GENEROSITY in September
FORGIVENESS in October
BALANCE OF MIND in November
CONTENTMENT in December

Imagine that you are in actual possession of the following virtues. Say to yourself, "I am patient. I will not get irritated from today. I will manifest this virtue in my daily life. I am improving." Think of the advantages of possessing the virtue of patience and the disadvantages of irritability. Introspect at the end of the day to find any digressions from its practice.

Adaptability
Adaptability is the ability to align with ever-changing circumstances. When the sense of ego is strong, adaptability is absent and we insist that the outside environment aligns itself with our ideas and desires. Adaptability sees beyond this and focuses on the greater good; it comes from an understanding that at the core of harmony is adaptability. That is dharma (nature and purpose) and it is the essence of creation.

Forgiveness
In forgiveness we release those we think have offended us from the obligation of what we think they owe us. We offer them a

healing hand and let them move forward. We make available good will so they can build a better future. Work on letting go of the past. Live in the future that you want to see, fashioned through your own power of thought and will. Let the past bury itself.

Fearlessness

Our true nature knows no fear. Love—where the perception of 'otherness' is absent—is the antidote to all fear. When we emphasize differences between others and ourselves the consequence will only be fear. Those who try to love and accept what they fear will fear no longer. Wherever there is love, there is no fear; wherever there is fear, there is no love. Love and fear cannot co-exist.

When we see nothing outside of ourselves then we are indeed fearless. Fearlessness is the abolition of all differentiation, all comparison, all 'otherness', all duality, all lovelessness. When we are truly united in our heart with someone, we do not fear them. Love knows no fear. The solution to all fear is love.

Gentleness

Gentleness, often misunderstood as weakness, brings joy to all of our relationships. Nowadays toughness or hardness is worshipped, and gentleness is no longer considered as a virtue to be nurtured. We want our heroes and heroines to have muscle and powerful weapons—they dominate our visual world; we see them daily in the movies and advertising. Gentleness is losing out! But not so in the case of a spiritual aspirant! Gentleness has the power to heal and conquer the heart of many, where weapons cannot. The power of gentleness is infinitely more subtle. Just as water erodes the hardest of rock so also gentleness wears away the crust of a closed heart. Its dharma is to bring healing and a smile. It manifests as softness of manners, gentle looks, kindness, deep understanding and love.

Giving

Through giving, life becomes a true blessing. To want something in return diminishes us into our tiny limited self and we feel pain, loneliness and suffering. Therefore expand and give, never asking, only giving. We are here only to give. Giving is one of the most sublime manifestations of love. It is nothing but the language of love. Love only begins and manifests where there is giving. Charity and spiritual life and the consequent expansion of the heart begin only by giving of our self. Practice giving with no reservation, no self-protection and no second thought. It is only through giving that we can forget our little self and enrich our own and others' lives. Give because it is sublime to give.

Gratitude

The power of gratitude is the power behind life and healing. Those who are grateful receive blessings and the limitless support of the vast creation, sustaining them from every direction. They are reborn every moment and the spring of creativity eternally flows in them. Gratitude allows us to feel the connection with all beneficial forces and entities within and without. It is the most important quality of an aspirant and is the cradle of humility, kindness, love and generosity. To be grateful is to earn the blessings of all those with whom we come in contact. Be grateful for every experience, as every experience is a precious teacher. Gratitude should be extended to all, since we are all interwoven in this incredible matrix of existence called life. Be grateful for the gifts even from those who may have caused you suffering—the lessons they taught you made you stronger, wiser, kinder and of sterner stuff. Every experience in life awakens us to the Reality, but is rarely seen as such. This includes all experiences, the sweetest, the happiest as well as the most painful and embarrassing. It is indeed a difficult practice, since it is so much easier to be grateful and feel the presence of Grace when things go well. But remember that every experience is calculated to balance, enrich or remedy. Every experience can be used as a compass for directing us to harmony. Life is magnificent, and even more magnificent is God, who breathes His own life into it. We must nurture gratitude at all times as it enlarges our heart and expands our perception of all possibility of life. There is a close relationship between gratitude and the presence of Grace.

Humility

Humility is the absence of self-importance, pretentiousness, arrogance, conceit and pride. When we are aware of the amazing power of the Divine or nature herself, which governs the whole universe including the one who is amazed, we cannot but be humble. When we see the impact of a negative karma we cannot help but feel a sense of wonder and respect for the intelligence that controls Creation. Humility does not in any way imply belittlement; humility enables us to eradicate our negative qualities and identify with all. If we meditate deeply on the transitory nature of this world and life, and reflect on the fleeting existence of our bodies and all our relationships, we can only be filled with deep awe and humility in our hearts.

Kindness

Kindness is the sister of mercy. We can only know kindness by continuously identifying with those who suffer; by remembering how painful it is to receive the unkindness of others; and by remembering the healing power of a smile, soft look or word, or even silence. Everyone in this life has inherited some form of suffering. A yogi builds a temple of the highest realization on the firm rock of foundation of ethics. Kindness is a form of love. It is a positive practice of ahimsa or love and one of the many facets of Oneness. It is to be lived in the smallest fractions of time and in the smallest measure of action. In expressing our kindness we honor and accept the aspect of vulnerability that plays such a large part in human nature. Kindness is found in those with a highly integrated mind and heart;

it is the expression of the gracefulness of the best of human nature, of our infinite potential to love.

Mercy

Mercy shines with even more brilliance than justice. The person of mercy serves and loves the person who has wronged him or her. Feel for others' sufferings. Be merciful in your judgment of others. Remember your own defects, frailties and weaknesses. Be slow in your criticism of others and generous towards those who do wrong actions. Show mercy to others. Others will be merciful to you. You will receive mercy when it shall be most needed. This is the immutable law of God.

Swami Sivananda

Mercy arises from the deep knowledge that one common life exists in all beings. Mercy is feeling the presence of another being in our own heart. Their suffering is our suffering. Their tearful eyes bespeak the pain we share, which at one time was ours and now is theirs. When we unite in our hearts with those that suffer, we help them embrace their torment in the warmth of our softness, love and acceptance so they may heal. We are gentle and patient with them just as we are when we watch a baby taking its first faltering steps. There are many baby souls on this earth walking with faltering steps towards the light and truth and we must support them in their struggle to find balance, regain faith and rediscover the love and the joy of being alive. There are also more mature souls who were once steeped in the darkness of the past, and who after a lengthy fight, rose to glory through unstinting effort and countless mistakes. How hard it is to walk the narrow path of truth, virtue and purity. Let us embrace all in our struggle to reach the final destination—that of freedom.

Patience

In this age of 'instant everything', we have lost our appreciation for and our control over time and as a consequence we have no patience—vegetables are forcibly ripened, children must learn rapidly, relationships are given no time to mature, and the long path to Self-realization is to be shortened! There are seasons in all undertakings; spring, summer, fall and winter exist in all phenomena. Keep up the practice and the enthusiasm and you will reap the reward.

Peace

Peace begins first within ourselves. Eliminate suspicion, prejudice and envy. Burn up the seeds of greed for power and possession. Lead a simple life. If we practice meditation daily and establish peace in our own heart, we radiate peace and contribute peace to the whole world. For any virtue to unfold, its seed must first be sown within our own mind and heart. Peace has its root in the unfathomable Awareness within. Without meditation, without reflection, without higher purpose, there can be no peace. All violence without will find its end when violence within is purged.

Refinement

Refinement is a golden adornment of a spiritual aspirant. Those who are refined are close to godliness. They exhibit graciousness in their manners, elegance in their movement, gestures and speech. Their attractive demeanor reflects great thoughtfulness and sensitivity. They have an eye for others' needs, for service, and they spontaneously act to make others happy and comfortable. Rich in dynamism, free from idleness and hastiness and with a nature thoroughly purified, they are adored by all. Their precision and softness in action is what we may call a spiritual elegance. They have banished all desire to harm and injure, or to gossip. They have made their mind free of all judgment. They walk and talk and yet they meditate in action. This refinement is not mechanically-exercised as found in the elite of societies, but is the result of control over thought and the practice of spiritual discernment.

Simplicity

Simplicity graces one who sees through the illusion of possession, greed and sense of ownership and the complexity that these bring in their wake. We come into this world with nothing, and we leave with nothing. What is to be owned in-between? Equally important and a manifestation of simplicity is to be established in the truth of our own being. Let us rid ourselves of falseness and hypocrisy, remaining in the pristine naturalness of who we are, like a child who shines in its own beauty. Let us live with no pretence to impress, not even to show off our so-called selfless nature, surrendering everything, all fruits, to the true owner, the Lord or Supreme Reality.

EXERCISE 1
TAKE FIVE EXERCISE

Write on paper five good qualities, using the examples below or others you wish to develop. The practice consists of generating the qualities and dwelling on them for one minute each. Total exercise time: five minutes. For each quality create a couple of lovely sentences—thoughts that you maintain and run through your mind throughout the exercise to help you generate the true experience of that particular quality. Use a memory of a similar experience you had in the past or think of one who is an embodiment of that quality and who inspires you to develop it. Charge the thoughts through imagination and feeling and let the power of that quality arise in your whole body, breath, heart and mind.

Calmness

I am calm and self-possessed; even in stress and in the heat of worldly duties I maintain calmness. Calmness is my true nature.

I can feel it now in my body, my breath, my look . . .
I take a deep breath and move into the next moment calmly,
and I move perhaps a little slower.
Contemplate the verse in the Bhagavad Gita:

*Just like a lamp placed in a windless spot does not flicker, this
state is comparable to the yogi, having controlled the mind, who
engages his self in yoga.*

Bhagavad Gita Ch VI v.19

Kindness

Kindness is my true nature. I express kindness in everything I
do, I say, I think and in the way I look.
I think of others with great love, kindness, compassion . . .
I place my steps in kindness.
I feel kindness vibrating in all my cells.
I breathe in kindness.

Fearlessness/Courage

I am free from fear here and now.
I smile and I walk fearlessly along the streets of this city.
I look with steady eyes . . . I talk confidently . . .
I feel great courage welling up in my chest now; I feel all the
cells in my body are bathing in the vibration of fearlessness.
I breathe in courage and breathe out fear.

Freedom

I am free here and now.
I express my freedom in the way I think and make decisions.
I am not distracted.
I am particularly free from worry; I do not worry.
I am free from unnecessary desires and longings.
I am free from unsattvic (impure) thoughts and desires.

Efficiency

Repeat these sentences before and when you work.
I am efficient with (my) time.
I am efficient with (my) energy. I conserve my energy.
My mind is organized and methodical in work.
I choose the most important among many thoughts.
I follow one line of thought, one activity at a time.
I feel the flow of thought and joy in any particular activity.

Use the same pattern with forgiveness, trust, openness and resolution, integrity, righteousness, wisdom, willpower, compassion, inner strength and firmness.

EXERCISE 2
MENTAL REPETITION OF A QUALITY

With your morning breathing exercises, repeat inwardly the word 'patience' or any other quality you wish to develop, immersing yourself in its meaning, its vibrations. While saying this word, add a meaningful image to it that will increase its power, with the result that this virtue will eventually fill your whole consciousness.

EXERCISE 3
FOR ONE WEEK: THINK OF STRENGTH

A deep hope, a constant positive thought and effort are the very essence of both a life well-lived and Self-realization. Think of and talk only about strength. Remind yourself daily that strength is your real nature. Encourage others to feel strength.

CHAPTER 17

SELF-REFLECTION AND
SPIRITUAL DIARY

Introspect. Look within. Try to remove all your defects. This is real and the most difficult sadhana (spiritual practice). You will have to do it at any cost. Mere intellectual development is nothing; it is easy. You can develop your intellect through study. But the former needs a great deal of struggle for many years. Success in meditation is not possible without eradication of these undesirable negative qualities of the lower nature.

Swami Sivananda

Just as a gardener protects and watches carefully over young plants making sure that they are watered and that weeds are removed, so also we must find out what it is that impedes our growth and prevents the light within us manifesting in full, and gradually weed out the thoughts of fear, anger and depression that undermine us. The gardener of the mind must learn the science of self-reflection or self-introspection.

Self-reflection is integral to self-development and mastery of the mind. Self-reflection goes under several names—self-introspection, self-analysis and self-observation. It is the ability to observe or witness our own feelings, thoughts, mental processes and conclusions, and think, with detachment, of the actions of our day and make adjustments accordingly. Self-reflection is not only a process of observation but involves using the discriminative portion of the mind to watch, examine and evaluate our thoughts, feelings and conduct. And at the same time we must contemplate our higher purpose in life and attune our minds and hearts to this vast creation and the divine laws behind the universe. The more we self-reflect the more refined and subtle our awareness becomes.

We cannot change our nature too quickly. Nature allows only for small steps, small increments of will. The practice of self-reflection allows us to make these small but transformational steps and even though the steps may not be giant, progress will be rapid. Reflection of events of today will give us greater clarity, purpose and will for the challenges of tomorrow. Our errors of judgment will gradually melt in the light of rising awareness, and the joy we feel will exceed any pleasure we may have had up till now. We become one of our own making; we can claim our own freedom, which will remain with us always. We will reinforce our good habits, and the negative aspects with which we still struggle to overcome will be easier to deal with subsequently. When we study the lives of great people we see that they have spent a great deal of time in self-observation, regularly 'checking' themselves in order to maintain their own standards of perfection, keeping a running mental inventory of their own actions.

Initially every act of control of the senses, speech or the mind means establishing a boundary or a restriction, and in the beginning of our practice, it may appear to be painful. The mind will have lost its toys in the form of lower pleasures but soon we feel great joy.

There is greater happiness in giving up a desire than in its fulfillment.

Buddha

We have come into this world to master certain qualities and to develop certain strengths. If we frequently become impatient, then our challenge and our lesson is to learn its opposite, to develop patience, forgiveness, acceptance and love; if our mind is fearful, our lesson is to develop courage; if we are prone to judging others we need to learn acceptance and kindness. Our task is to free up and strengthen the will, and perfect our love. Strength of will is connected to self-control and mastery of love takes place when all selfishness is removed.

The mind is a great magician, capable of the greatest trickeries. To conduct precise and effective self-reflection, it is advisable to focus, not on negative qualities alone, but on the pure, divine element within us all—that part of us which is made of light and which we may call the higher mind or Self. This is the source of all our compassion and love. It is this innermost part of us that cares deeply for ourselves. It is that which also represents the best part of ourselves, and it is rightfully our best judge and guide. This part of our being knows the truth, it is filled with wisdom and love and its main concern is to lead us on, higher and higher, in the ascent to the Ultimate Goal. It is only in the light of this awareness, in its warm and compassionate embrace, that we should examine all our actions, feelings and thoughts. With the help of this great, insightful and wise part of ourselves, we can make conclusions about our actions.

The spiritual path is rugged, thorny and precipitous. The feet may become tired and bruised. The heart may pant. But the reward is very great. You will become immortal. Persevere. Plod on diligently. Be on the alert. Be agile and nimble like the squirrel. There are no resting places on the path. Hear the small inner voice. It will guide you if you are pure and sincere.

Swami Sivananda

The best time to reflect on our actions is at night and it should be done daily. You will soon make amazing discoveries about your mind—how and where it wanders, what it is attracted to, what it is disturbed by, and so on. Such self-analysis will invariably reveal the inner contents of the mind and the ways in which we can amend negative emotions and thoughts. Start with a few minutes and see if you can increase the practice to about half an hour each night. Watch how your thoughts form into more solidified opinions and judgements about persons and events. Go through your day and think of the actions you have done, the thoughts you had, the conclusions you made. Ask yourself, "Why have I come to that particular conclusion? Was that the right one?" Self-reflection is a rewarding exercise. In due course this itself will become a meditation; you will also discover methods for overcoming your problems.

No self-reflection can be considered adequate without the help of a spiritual diary. The power and importance of keeping a spiritual diary is inestimable.

The keeping of a daily spiritual diary is of paramount importance for a serious spiritual aspirant. The diary is your teacher and guide. It is an eye-opener. It will help you destroy all your negative qualities and to be regular in your spiritual practices. It shows the way to freedom and Eternal Bliss. Those who wish to evolve rapidly should keep a diary. You will get solace, peace of mind and quick progress on the spiritual path.

Swami Sivananda

When we wish for the mind or behavior to change we focus on others—how they act or shouldn't act—but actually our concern should be only with our own mind. When in good spirits and optimistic we are happy to make plans for our practice, we have the desire to improve. We are confident, convinced that we will keep our resolutions and walk vigorously on the path of light. What we don't bargain for is how quickly the mind can change—what was enthusiasm a moment ago can transform in a flash to despair. We don't foresee the obstacles that may arise in the course of a day and when they do appear we are taken by surprise, we lose our enthusiasm and despair overwhelms us; we forget the intention we made. The diary will help us overcome this tendency.

The diary shows us how to eradicate obstacles and negative traits and to bring life to our full potential. It is extremely difficult to understand the mind, by nature as quick as lightning, deceptive and slippery. It is not easy for us, without some point of reference and without objectivity, to know ourselves well. Even if we have undergone lengthy training under a master it may still remain a challenge. The majority of us have no teacher and as a consequence our minds are held under the sway and spell of the two gunas or qualities, tamas (inertia) and rajas (restlessness, impetuousness). Each guna has its own language, as it were, and mode of manifestation. *Tamo-guna*— or inertia—can be seen as lack of discriminative power, lack of willpower, general ignorance or blindness, manifesting as a justification of action based on instinct and primordial drive. *Rajo-guna* thrives on its own projections and is permeated with desire of all kinds, greed and ego. The gunas are an integral part of our nature and it is trying to say the least for most of us to extricate and isolate our awareness from their influence, from the tremendous pull that these two powerful forces exert; it is taxing and challenging to judge accurately the state of our own mind.

The object of spiritual practice is to generate *Sattva-guna*, the quality of luminescence and embracing awareness, sharp, razor-like intelligence full of kindness and which acts as an inner teacher. Initially it is to be found in our external teacher or master. By observing them, and through their kindness and training, we learn how slowly to cultivate the sattva guna within ourselves. The teacher acts as a point of reference and a mirror of our actions, and as an ideal to emulate. You may have a teacher or you may not. But in the absence of the teacher, this is exactly what a spiritual diary does—it teaches us how to awaken the sattva guna within. Nothing can replace a teacher, yet keeping a spiritual diary will awaken our inner sattva, our intuition, the teacher within. It teaches us to be accurate in perceiving how we act, what our thoughts and feelings are and yet to remain kind and creative at the same time.

Why have so many of us kept a diary or journal at some time in our lives, often without knowing the reason? Because each time we write down our thoughts, we are off-loading our subconscious mind and we become, at least to some degree, clearer about the nature of the experience or problem about which we are writing. We develop a better understanding of ourselves. So many of us are under the illusion that we know ourselves well, simply because we are so preoccupied with our thoughts and actions. However, this preoccupation has very little to do with the truth. We believe we know the mind so well that we have no need to record our thoughts. But we underestimate the power of the mind's undercurrents and we find ourselves in unexpected emotional turmoil or in mental stagnation.

The mind is vast and incomprehensible with countless hidden nooks and crannies—it would do us well to admit that we know very little of our minds. We must develop humility, it is the most important step we can make. We appear to have two natures that are continually in conflict, the higher and lower. We also have two images; the image we have of ourselves and the image that others see. They don't often match! We can think we are free of a particular negative quality that in fact we do have. It is hard for us to admit that we fall short of our ideals. We may believe for example that we are generous or kind but if asked we might be hard pushed to recall the last time we acted in such a way! Remember that the mind easily forgets spiritual and psychological goals but does not forget to go to a meeting for work or join up with a friend. The nature within resists!

A spiritual aspirant must be a good psychologist and the diary lays the foundation for that knowledge. The diary will helps us to increase awareness of our mental state, thoughts, emotions, desires and more. It deepens our understanding of the mind and its potential. There is no better friend nor more faithful teacher than our diary. With a spiritual diary we will see clearly how frequently we indulge in angry, self-deprecating or worrying thoughts, much more than we thought we did and how wide the gap is between what we think and what we do. We will see clearly how irregular are our patterns of living. Perhaps our eating schedule is erratic or we go to sleep or wake up at a different hour each day. We will be astonished at how much we have underestimated the power of our own mind, the great trickster in hiding!

The diary shows us the impact of the unpredictable nature and changing circumstances of life and with its help we can keep our practice regular and steady. It helps us rectify many of our weaknesses and evolve quickly and shows us whether we are making progress. It is important to see our own progress—the more we advance in spiritual work, the greater are the chances to be led astray by pride or temptation and the greater the necessity for maintaining a diary. The diary connects us to the truth of where we stand; it allows us to look at ourselves with honesty, without feeling guilt or recrimination. Unknowingly we waste a tremendous amount of energy in concealing our own shortcomings.

Guidelines for keeping a spiritual diary:

- Maintain a resolve form along with the diary. Give yourself definite goals, but avoid setting them too high. At the end of the day compare how far you were able to execute your resolves. You can renew your efforts—to do even better the following day! Gradually within a few days or weeks, through mistakes and failings, you will reach your desired goal. You can then increase a particular practice.

• Do not be anxious about your progress. The diary can give you a great deal confidence provided that you are gentle with yourself.

• We think that something has to be wrong in order for us to change. With a diary we are able to make changes without seeing ourselves as inherently bad. There must be a certain level of acceptance; changes occur faster if we are self-accepting, humble and not in denial of what needs to change.

• The diary helps in visible and invisible ways. Write all the details of your practice; even if you did none on a particular day and you have to write zeroes, it will still be helpful. However poor the record may be, it is better to have it than none. It is a good idea if you carry your diary with you and check it a few times a day.

• Experiment with different spiritual practices, virtues and vows. You will discover your strengths as well as weaknesses in regard to them.

• If you have a teacher, send them a copy of your diary on a weekly basis. This will strengthen your commitment to the practice.

• If you don't have a teacher, perhaps share your experience of keeping a diary with a close friend or partner who also keeps a diary. Both parties need to keep their own diary. You can then have valuable discussions about the successes and challenges of different practices weekly or monthly, creating new approaches to your practices and at the same time inspiring one another.

Create a spreadsheet for the spiritual diary. Use the example here to guide you. Do not demand too many practices of yourself. Small changes and small victories are the sign of true success. For example, if you see that your asana practice is irregular and your wish is to do thirty minutes each day but you can't seem to manage it, then start by doing five minutes a day—but every day. You will feel encouraged and will gradually strengthen and will soon taste the sweet fruit of self-victory. The same principle applies to working with any emotion, habit or tendency. A small but powerful plan is the tool for evolution. Remember that nature does not allow for sudden change. All growth is gradual. Be honest with yourself. Write down exactly the type of practices you managed and any other details you might wish to record. At the end of each week or month calculate the total number of hours you have spent in your asana practice, study of spiritual books, breathing exercises.

Once you maintain a daily diary properly, you will come to understand the value of time and how it slips away. A spiritual diary will not let you relax your efforts; it will chase you like a tiger; it will follow right behind your heels; it will bite you if you stop. Just as you think to give up a practice, it is at that point that the diary is a great savior. It will not allow you to indulge in any kind of self-justification. The diary is a terrific friend, even if sometimes scary to have around. It is a whip, a terrible reminder of our slackness, of time passing and of opportunities lost, and of ill destiny succumbed to. It will tell you untiringly that you had better be real, honest and understand clearly the purpose of your life; it honors only self-effort. It knows no excuses, it laughs at them; it knows all your secrets and failings; it is your guru, completely detached yet supremely compassionate—it is the voice of God. It annihilates the belief that life is predestined. It will convince you that you can succeed. It will unfold the divine within you. It will suggest ways and techniques for mastering the mind in matters previously beyond your reach. It is supremely patient; it watches as you leave blanks, evidence of practice not done, and waits calmly until you can muster your will.

Carefully observe the ways of the mind. It tempts, exaggerates, magnifies, infatuates, unnecessarily alarms through vain imagination, vain fear, vain worries and vain forebodings. It tries its level best to divert you from your object of your concentration.

Swami Sivananda

A spiritual diary cannot be maintained, nor mastery over the mind achieved, without vows. Vows are deep intentions, energies and aspirations. They form an integral part of discipline behind training of the mind. As seed energies, the vows are deposited deeply in the subconscious mind and through its power work to bring about the required result. They are present in our dreams and on an unconscious level in our waking state. There are good and bad vows. When we experience anger we may 'take' a bad vow such as refusing to talk to someone. Good vows contribute greatly to making you into a perfect human being. Think of your vows as soon as you get up and often during the day. Here are some examples to guide you:

- I will be patient.

- I will show kindness to others.

- I will not interrupt others in their conversation.

- I will remember to repeat my mantra.

- I will focus on the breath every half hour for at least three minutes.

- I will keep balance of mind.

- I will speak only good things about others.

- I will keep my thoughts pure and positive.

- I will remain cheerful throughout the day.

- I will cultivate compassion for ALL beings.

- I will be fearless.

- I will serve others.

- I will observe simplicity and humility in my manners.

- I will discipline my mind.

- I will talk less but meaningfully and sweetly.

- I will think of others first.

- I will practice forgiveness; I will be tolerant.

- I will practice truthfulness.

- I will not hurt anyone.

- I will keep my word.

Make only resolves that you can carry out. If you make too many initially it will be like overloading a weak muscle. Discipline should be slow and gradual. Make realistic resolves and use them along with your diary.

EXERCISE 1
RETRACING STEPS

In the evening, go back through the day, remembering at least the last ten to fifteen actions which you did prior to going to bed (sequentially, follow their order backwards) and see if there were some that you could have avoided or changed. Due to impulsiveness and lack of discrimination we may have done something that left us feeling agitated and restless. With the simple question, "Why?" watch the answers unfold. Correct your way of acting so that the following day you will be both more aware and vigilant if a tendency to repeat the behavior arises. Then look at your good actions, those that you consider to have been done well, appreciating your judgment and your ability to act according to your best standards of thought and action. Clarity in the ability to see what needs to be addressed and the commitment to try harder is the key to this method.

EXERCISE 2
NEW PATHWAYS (COGNITIVE METHOD)

At the end of the day for at least ten minutes, watch the mind, as a witness. Watch your thoughts in relation to the events of the day. Pay attention particularly to the negative thoughts you may have had about yourself, other people or events. Imagine that a part of the mind—the observing part which is peaceful and non-reactive—is now watching the judgmental, emotional and reactive part of the mind. For practical reasons we may call the former the higher or discriminative mind, but the more accurate word would be awareness. Gently coax your mind to abandon negative ways of seeing and thinking, suggesting to it new and positive approaches. It will then be freed from impulsive, emotional entanglement, allowing clarity and understanding to flourish.

EXERCISE 3
INTROSPECTION LIST

Create a sheet with questions on the values that you consider most important, and briefly answer them. This will widen your understanding of how you act and grow. The introspection list may include the following questions:

- Did I do my spiritual practices today?

- Did I respect my body? Did I eat well? Did I exercise? Did I go to sleep on time?

- Did I greet people with kindness and respect?

- Did I contemplate Nature?

- Did I express gratitude to life? Did I offer any gifts?

- Did I show lack of discrimination?

- Did I make good use of my freedom of choice? If not, why?

- What was the greatest temptation in exercising my will?

- What should I do next time?

- Did I waste time? If yes, why?

- Did I despise or talk ill of anybody? If yes, why?

SPIRITUAL DIARY

Week from_____ to_____

	Plan	Mon	Plan	Tue	Plan	Wed	Plan	Thu	Plan	Fri	Plan	Sat	Plan	Sun	Total
GENERAL SADHANA															
What time did I wake up?															
How much time did I spend sleeping?															
How long did I meditate in the morning?															
How long did I do asanas?															
How long did I do pranayama?															
How long did I meditate in the evening?															
How long did I do Japa?															
How long did I spend in Swadhyaya?															
How long in Satsang?															
How long in Karma Yoga?															
How much time did I waste today?															
When did I go to sleep?															
SPEECH SADHANA															
How many lies told?															
How many times did I interrupt others or try to monopolize the conversation?															
How many times did I show respect to others in the form of politeness and gentleness?															
How long in Mauna?															
ETHICAL SADHANA															
Quality to meditate on and develop:															
Quality to eradicate this week:															
What counter-action did I apply this week each time I failed?															
How many times did I fail in Brahmacharya?															
RESOLUTION FOR THIS WEEK:															
(check when done, put minus when not done)															

Commentary:

187

CHAPTER 18

THE BREATH OF INSPIRATION

MASTER OF DESTINY

If destiny is the effort of yesterday, the future is created by the effort of today. How we use our free will today will become our future. We have free will; we are free to act. Action takes place first on the level of thought. Make full use of your freedom of choice; it is there available moment by moment. What may seem difficult to alter in our life now is simply the result of the greater effort that was made in that particular direction in the past. Let us make greater effort now in the direction of what we want to become. To know this law is the path to freedom. You are the master of your destiny.

ENTERING THE PATH OF LIGHT

OM Dear Spiritual Traveller! The most important decision you have made in life is to have entered the path of Light. Take a deep breath and congratulate yourself! This is no small achievement! To come closer to the Inner Self, God or simply Light is the greatest of achievements. All others will evaporate into an airy nothing. No light is ever seen without first knowing darkness. For many of you, who have perhaps arrived at the Golden Gate of a new beginning, have done so through a long journey filled with moments of darkness, desperation, desolation and great struggle. The night is always darkest before the arrival of the dawn. Do not mind the past and the mistakes you may have committed. Stay strong in your commitment to working and being in Light. The Light will support you! Let your heart be nourished by unceasing inspiration to serve, love, give, purify, meditate and realize.

FIRE OF INSPIRATION

Inspiration is the heartbeat of a yogi. It is the mystical voice of hope of the Soul within. It is the inner fire of the sun-like spirit coursing through our veins and nourishing our most sublime thoughts. Inspiration is the language of the heart, the language of love and faith. We are inspired only by what we learn to know and love. Inspiration opens new avenues and accomplishes greatness. Inspiration turns obstacles into stepping stones to success. It is this fire of inspiration that must be protected and carefully nurtured. When it is tended with care the path is lit with the great light of Spirit and that luminescence reveals to us how to work with the impediments and obstacles of life. Let the river of inspiration never go dry.

NEVER MIND THE STRUGGLE

All warriors on the path of Light! It is a day of celebration! You have been granted another opportunity, given another day to become the master of your thoughts, to overcome all desires but one—that of liberation, to be free of the desires that have tied you down in the land of lost freedom and darkness. Each day is a call to find the true meaning of your life and sing the glories of your real, beautiful Self, the God within you. A new day is the day to conquer the yet unconquered, to gain sovereignty over this seemingly indomitable mind. Never mind the struggle. Struggle is the very essence of spiritual life. It is the one thing needed before you enter into the Effortlessness. Never mind the falls as long as you keep your head up and keep walking towards the Light.

SEEK THE PATH OF TRUTH

Diligently seek the path of truth; tread it carefully and vigilantly, for you may slip and fall. On this unchartered territory your real guru (preceptor) is your own heart—he is the indweller, the inner ruler. Longing for final liberation is the hunger for the spiritual food of knowledge of the eternal.

Swami Sivananda

Those who are diligent will reap the fruits of their labor. Diligence is the price of liberation. A fall is nothing if one can rise again. Darkness cannot overwhelm one who is enamored of light. Where the true voice of the Divine is heard is in the innermost recesses of the heart. Enter them daily for a bath in the ambrosia of bliss.

TO LIGHTEN YOUR PATH

Remember the great Law—like attracts like. Use the same force or nature, of the very quality which you want to achieve. Great is this law!

Life animates life.
Light enkindles light.
Smile evokes smile.
Kindness kindles kindness.
Love engenders love.
Hatred promotes hatred.
Faith encourages deeper faith.
Effort draws new effort.

TOLERANCE

Tolerance is the law of life and integration. It is another word for love. Intolerance is the seed of hatred, destruction and disintegration. Tolerance begins at home, with ourselves. Our greatest need is to learn the art of self-acceptance. Let us learn to live without judgment of any kind, and be free from the little condemnatory voice within that is ever-busy in making us feel inadequate, wrong or lost. Let us embrace—without judgment and free from any self-imposed stigma—our body with its idiosyncrasies and our mind with its emotions and moods. Let us learn to accept the painful memories, failures, hurts and changes that have taken place without our understanding, wish or knowledge. We are all in need of daily nourishment and contact with the Changeless within our heart. In the early hours of the day let us feel the power of the Great Silence and sense immense love welling up. They will stand like a buffer against all the vicissitudes of the ever-changing circumstance of life.

191

STRENGTH

Think of strength. Meditate on strength. Remind yourself constantly of your infinite strength. Live with strength. Sing the song of strength. Walk in strength. Talk of strength. Why think small, when you are the emperor of this vast kingdom, your life and this creation? Why recount the events of the past and of things you have lost, of people that may have hurt or betrayed you? Why ruminate over lost loves and opportunities? Why think, "I can't do it."? Learn from the ocean. Ask the ocean, "What can you teach me today?" And then listen attentively! And you will hear, "I teach you by my silent presence of the infinite strength that exists within you! Follow my path! That of strength!"

SAY NO TO THE MEDIOCRE

Never settle for the ordinary or mediocre. For many the ordinary is within easy reach and is for those who want only a little pleasure and comfort in this life. But you, my friend, are meant to go the full distance, to the very entrance of Eternal Freedom and Peace. Freedom is your birthright. Freedom is the very reason you were born, to reclaim it, to own it. Sovereignty is your heart. Your domain of rulership is your mind and the grand ruler of everything is the Inner Self or Atman. Remember always that Freedom is the realization of the Oneness of all.

TRANSFORMATION

To turn our demons into angels and our sharp stones into precious diamonds is a form of alchemy. True spiritual aspirants are alchemists, able to transform everything to their own advantage for their own growth. This 'magic' requires tremendous vigilance, humility, faith and willpower. Every situation is an opportunity to apply spiritual principles, to strengthen a weakness, to remove a negative quality, or simply to help. Every opportunity carries a seed of enlightenment. Life is full of small steps, infinite beginnings and awesome possibilities. Take life's gift and open your heart. Constantly aspire to reach new heights in your love, understanding, knowledge and realization and from today vow to have no despair, no worry, and no fear.

CHOOSE YOUR THOUGHT

Assert your freedom by learning to think by choice. Freedom of thought is the ability to steer the mind, like a boat in the ocean of life, in the direction of wisdom and kindness. There may be storms, ignore them and keep guiding the mind towards the rising sun of supreme wisdom and joy. Free the mind from all unnecessary thought which constitutes most of our thinking. How often do we experience an emptiness in the course of life, an unoccupied moment, a few minutes, sometimes more. And what do we do? Immediately we distract ourselves, and invent some foolishness or other to pass the time. Our way to escape from boredom is to act foolishly. Go daily into the Silence behind all thought where there are no desires, no 'what next?'

THINK YOURSELF GREAT

Establish yourself in the understanding that the mind alone is responsible for ALL experiences. Train the mind to understand that the process of thinking brings about its own consequences and that all thoughts materialize. Such knowledge can quickly lead you to the highest realization. Within the infinite waves of life there are infinite possibilities, numerous opportunities to make yourself what you will. Think of your life as pure blessing. Yes! We know not that we are sitting on a treasure trove! Realize what you are in reality. Do not let your mind think small. Do not let your imagination diminish you. Think yourself great, noble and deserving.

OM TAT SAT